Live Your Life As Good As It Gets (Don't Throw Away Those Dreams of Success)

By Matthew Bradley

Edited by Adam Cardy

First Printing, 2017

Printed by Lulu

Printed in the United States of America

ISBN 978-0-244-60228-4

All photos by Matthew Bradley

Front and back cover design by Matthew Bradley

Live your life as good as it gets (Don't throw away those dreams of success)

CONTENTS

Chapter One

'So let me introduce to you...'

Nostalgia, a forgotten memory that creeps into your head and instantly takes you back to when life was care free, hopes and dreams still had realistic meaning and expectations were astronomical. I had a good upbringing. I grew up in Port Talbot, an industrial town, a few miles from Swansea, South Wales. I came from a good, loving home, which I shared with my parents, John and Lorna and my older brothers John and Mike. I wanted for nothing as a child. Both my parents worked hard, so life was comfortable. I had regular holidays and happy memories, although, I often found myself in trouble with the neighbours, at school, and even the police. I suppose in today's world, I would be diagnosed with some form of Attention Deficit Hyperactivity Disorder, or some other ridiculous name given to a child that back then was just known as a naughty little bastard. Obviously there must have been some concern about my misdemeanours, as I have vague memories of visiting a child psychologist or behaviour therapist. I was playing with toys while he observed my behaviour and scribbled on a piece of paper. To this day I wonder what his diagnosis was. Spawn of Satan? Another child failed by modern society destined for the dole line forever? Christ, I was only 6! I'll never know what he wrote down but in reality, I was a quiet, polite and well-mannered young boy, with the occasional tendency to sporadically have a complete and utter melt down. To me, this was normal behaviour.

In the summer of 1990, England had just been knocked out of the football World Cup at the semi-finals held in Italy by West Germany. Gazza's tears at the end of the penalty shootout would go on to become legendary. I was 6 years old. My dad was a welder in the local steel works. My mother was an auxiliary nurse at Port Talbot Hospital. I was very close to my mother as a child, I still I am, but back then I was glued to her hip. My earliest of memories were eagerly anticipating a rare bus journey over the old Beach Hill and looking forward to that turn you got in your stomach once you were over the dip. Apart from the occasional trip in a vehicle, we appeared to seemingly walk everywhere, from our home in Sandfields, to the town centre, to Margam Park and back again, occasionally stopping off at Lens Fish Shop for rissole and chips. For the early part of my life I thought we were Nomads. As most kids would, I tended to push boundaries more with my mother than I would with my dad. One afternoon, I wanted to go fishing with my older friends, down the Swan Lake about a mile from my house. A few days before, I was bought a fishing rod from the Eric's sports shop on Victoria Road, even though I had no idea how to actually fish, I was excited to try it out. My friends came over to ask if I could go with them, but my mother refused. I was like the Incredible Hulk back then, and the green mist set in, Being the little shit that I was, I responded by punching the kitchen window through. There was glass everywhere. I immediately ran away in a fit of rage, though I soon returned, begging my mother not to tell my dad. I knew I'd have a sore arse for weeks if I was on the receiving end of one of his slaps. Somehow my mother managed to find a glazer who could replace the entire window before my dad returned from work. Luckily for me, my dad never found out about that, probably until now. I'll probably still get that slap. My eldest brother, John, was in the army and had just been posted out to the first Gulf War. My other brother, Mike, worked for a local company called Rhino Doors; he travelled throughout the country with his work. One morning, I was downstairs enjoying my breakfast when I heard Mike calling out

6

in pain for my mother. My Mam went up to investigate and found that Mike had broken his ribs as the result of a motorcycle accident. Apparently, he had lost control of a friend's bike and smashed into a lamppost. He was very lucky that he escaped with nothing worse than a few broken ribs and a bruised ego. It would later transpire that being reckless appeared to run through the family. It was also around this time when my parents took me rugby training for the first time off the back of my visit to the behaviour therapist. It had been decided that my issue was indeed, hyperactivity, and that a contact sport would do me the world of good. To my knowledge, I had no prior interest in rugby, but I found the sport came very natural to me. I maintain that my athletic appetite stemmed from the area that I grew up in. I had always been an active child, rarely indoors, I was always down Vivian Park with the boys from Seabrook Place, Christopher O'Leary, Donald O'Leary, Daniel Andrews, Damian Adams and Shaun Wilkins. We would spend hours playing football, one and off, three and in, sometimes even fifteen players to each side but no matter what the score, we played to the golden rule, it was always, next goal wins. If we were not playing football, we were running amok around the surrounding streets, bobby door knocking, which basically means you knock someone's door, wait for them to open it, and then run like your life depends on it (in a later story, it would). Hide and seek was another game that could go on for hours as Vivian Park had a large area of bushes and trees to hide in. As a lot of kids do, we had got into the habit of setting fire to things, not maliciously, just rubbish bins, bits of old papers and the occasional post box. It seems crazy now, but back then we didn't have the luxury that kids have today. No PlayStations or IPads, we didn't even have mobile phones. We made our own fun and occasionally our own fun was breaking boundaries or even the law. One afternoon, I was in my bedroom with Chris O'Leary, I had found an old lighter in my brother's bedroom. I was like a caveman who'd just discovered fire for the first time, lighting the flame and adjusting it to make it larger. I'll never know what compelled me, but the sight of this flame and my net curtains nearby became too great a chance to ignore. I edged the flame closer to the curtain until, 'Whoosh,' the whole thing went up in seconds. It was terrifying and brilliant at the same time. My mind soon turned to my parents finding out. I ran downstairs to inform my mother of the fire burning itself out in my room. She stormed upstairs and demanded to know what happened. I had no hesitation in saying, "Christopher did it with a lighter." We were kept apart for a while after that, as he was considered a bad influence on me. Sorry Chris. Of the boys mentioned, in later life fooling around would eventually turn into crime. Both Donald and Daniel would spend time in and out of prison. I don't necessarily think they were bad people. In fact, I know they are not bad people. I'm still in touch with Donald and he is a lovable rogue and it's good to know he's turned his life around. I have not seen Daniel for years. I think both just fell afoul of the environment and circle of friends they were brought up with. As you can imagine, the odds appeared to be stacked against me if I'd kept this behaviour through to my teenage years. To this day, I'm not exactly sure what compelled me to steal from my neighbours garden and in some ways I'm glad of what happened next because I could never have made a good thief, I kept getting caught. I have vivid memories of climbing through a hole in the fence, as I had spotted a brand new Mitre Delta football, after happening to accidentally peer over the wall - a wall that was ten foot high I may add. After acquiring the aforementioned football, I became aware of a voice, followed by the outline of a person. What follows would not look out of place on a BBC wildlife programme. I quickly made my exit, back through the hole in the fence, like a gazelle chased by a lion, with my would-be attacker in hot pursuit. I'd almost made it to the sanctuary of my front garden when I was caught. A verbal dressing down was given and more than likely, a slap. Unbeknown to me at the time, this person would go on to become my best friend and a major influence in my life. Adam was a few years older than me, quieter, but we got on. Adams parents were divorced, and as he lived with his dad, Ian, on the other side of the town, I only saw him when he visited his mother, usually on Tuesday and Thursday nights. It was just a normal childhood friendship. We liked football, wrestling and computer games. If the weather was nice we would be out playing, if not, we would spend entire days playing on the Sega Mega Drive. The classics, Golden Axe or Double Dragon were the games of choice back then. As we got older, our influence on each other would grow. At the age of ten, I still wasn't really into music, that it to say, I didn't have the vast musical collection I have today. For my tenth birthday I got my first music system. It was a Sanyo CD player with a tape cassette. I also got four CDs - Born To Be Wild, Abba Gold, Bon Jovi's Greatest Hits; Crossroads and Now 29. That is quite the mix of genres. Back then you didn't have the likes of ITunes, YouTube or Spotify; your taste consisted on what you were given or what your parents listened too. Luckily for me, my parents played a lot of 60s' music and mainly on Saturday night. My Saturday evenings back then were spent visiting my Nan, while my parents had their weekly night out in the local Labour Club. My Nan was a very religious lady, who came from a large family. She could recite the names of her brothers and sisters in order of birth, some feat considering there were eleven of them. For years, these evenings ran like clockwork. Vegetable soup to start, then a large beef roll, crisps, one of those wafer chocolates that according to the wrapper sell four millions bars every week, but I don't know anybody else who buys them and, finally, a homemade pasty, not to mention three or four pints of fizzy orange pop in between. I was there for no more than four hours! I loved the food at my nans, it was a taste I've not experienced anywhere since. At around midnight my parents would pick me up on the way home from the club. The walk home was always eventful, my dad, a big Manchester United fan, would sing at the top of his voice for most of the short journey home, only stopping to point at three particular stars in the sky that were slightly out of line, if they were visible, and tell me that was my grandad looking down at us. I never met my grandad as he had passed away a few years before I was born but by all accounts, he was a remarkable man. Occasionally my Dad would mention that he was a better rugby player than me. This would usually result in us attempting to rugby tackle each other like rutting stags trying to establish dominance. One night, we both ended up falling into a neighbours bush after play fighting. We must have lay there for ten minutes after, laughing uncontrollably, while my mother stood over us calling us a 'pair of silly buggers'. These were great times. Once in the house, my dad, who had obviously had a few drinks by this point of the evening, would tell me to put the CD player on. More often than not, it was the classic hits of the 60s. My dad would close his eyes and declare his love for a particular song while appearing to be in some sort of trance while playing the imaginary guitar. My mother would venture in from the kitchen after making a compulsory late night sandwich and would sing every song while dancing around. She also liked recounting the story of how the doctors had told her that she would be too old to have another child, but a conversation with the local priest convinced her to keep me. I think she made the right decision. In March, 1994, my parents went away for the weekend to Paris to celebrate their wedding anniversary. I was put in the care of my brother, Michael. Two events stand out from this weekend. The first was Michael flooding the kitchen with mashed potato. I take it my brother was not used to cooking as he emptied the entire tub of instant mash into a bowl. Once the water was added and mixed in, it began to overflow at rapid speed. It was all over the worktop, up the walls, on the floor, it looked like an explosion in a paint factory. Mike salvaged what he could and served it to me. The second event was Michael then paying the eleven year old paper girl, who was in the middle of her round, to come in and clean the house before my parents returned home. I must say, she did a fantastic job as the kitchen and living room looked spotless. Well worth the one pound he paid her anyway. It was a good weekend; we spent to two days just playing football in the living room, using the sofa as the goal, and also watching dial MTV. Life was simple then. I went to the local catholic school, St Joseph's. I had a good group of friends. Funnily enough, a boy in my class, Jason Evans, had also had the Bon Jovi album for Christmas. We would spend entire days singing each song in order. This must have driven the teacher mad as we were constantly sent out of class. We didn't mind because we could rehearse without being disturbed in the corridor. We must have thought we were good because we entered the school talent show. Instead of sticking with our well-rehearsed tribute to Bon Jovi, we opted instead for a more popular song in the charts at the time. Using the ropes from the climbing frame as microphones, we got up and delivered a perfect performance of the Wet, Wet, Wet classic, 'Love Is All Around.' How we didn't win is still the biggest travesty is St Josephs Junior School history. Away from school, when I wasn't out playing with my friends, I was at a sports class, usually Rugby. I had joined the Aberavon Green Stars that play down on the Little Warren area of Port Talbot. The ground was on the beach front, with the docks running alongside it. Even in summer, temperatures never seemed to reach double figures, and in the winter it never rose above freezing. It was always gale force winds, driving rain and hailstones like golf balls. The authorities wouldn't even send convicted criminals out in that weather but this is where my parents, and others like them, deemed it a good idea to send their kids, every Thursday evening and Sunday morning and place them in shorts and t-shirt to brave the elements. To this day, I don't really feel the cold weather, and I put it down to the years of cold weather training that the SAS would struggle with, let alone little people of six years of age. It was a decent little team with a good balance. We were well coached by David Locke, Phil Jenkins, Tony Hanford and my dad. During a game against South Gower, I actually scored eight tries in one game. I'm sure this is still some sort of junior record. I was also fortunate enough to win numerous player of the year awards. It was my first introduction to team discipline and I'm sure the coaches from back then would agree that being told what to do didn't come naturally to me. By my own admittance, I must have been horrendous to control and I will forever be grateful that those mentioned persevered with me.

(Above) Me and my brother Michael.

(Above) My dad, Michael, me and John

(Below) My brother John's during his passing out parade for the army. My mam and me

Chapter Two

'The dreams we have as children...'

In the summer of 1994, I had just returned from holidaying in Majorca with my parents. Brazil had just won the football World Cup, beating Italy on penalties. I had my first crush on a children's entertainer at the resort, even going as far as to get up and dance just to get close to her, which today is unthinkable. I was effectively still a child but all that would soon change. I was in the car with my brother Michael; he had a light green mini back then. Both he and my eldest brother, John, were keen weightlifters and the sight of two large men in a tiny mini was quite a thing. A few years later, Mike would own a Peugeot 205 GTI, black, with leather seats. It was my childhood dream car. It would appear that others were also envious of the car, as one evening, somebody threw paint stripper over the bonnet and a few months later, the car was written off completely after being crashed into by a stolen vehicle.

To this day I can remember exactly where I was when I first heard a band that would go a long way to changing my teenage years. I was sat in my brother's car on St Paul's Road listening to Tom Petty and the Heartbreakers, while waiting for his friend to come out of the house. Mike changed the cassette and a song I had never heard before came on, I instantly liked it. The song in question was 'Columbia' by Oasis, it was like a seismic event in my head and from that moment on I followed the band religiously. I would wait until Mike bought their latest CD then steal it for myself. My infatuation grew. Today, three years doesn't seem like a great amount of time but back then, it was the start of an individual revolution. Myself and Adam, the kid whose football I'd tried to steal, began to distance ourselves over the following months from other friends and would spend hours listening to music. I'm glad he followed my taste as he had recently bought the Michael Jackson single, 'You Are Not Alone', and quite frankly, I feared which way he was going, plus growing up could have been very different for me. It was Oasis rivalry with fellow Brit pop group, Blur that really made Oasis a household name. In 1995 a chart war broke out, Oasis released the single, 'Roll with It', while Blur released 'Country House.' Such was the frenzy that the story actually made headline news in the UK. Blur would eventually go on to win that particular battle, but it was Oasis who would win the war. The bands dual captivated us and we obsessed about forming our own band in the future. The only problem we had with that idea was, there were only two of us and the only instrument I had was an electric drum machine in my bedroom that actually belonged to my brother and I couldn't even play that. He had got the drum machine after collecting a huge number of tokens in the cigarette pack of Embassy Number 1. We would talk about growing up and for some bizarre reason, would sit on top of the concrete bus stop roof, opposite my mam's house. By now I was 12 and had started comprehensive school at St Josephs. By my own admission, school was never my top priority. I had started to grow my hair, listened to Britpop, which was rapidly taking over the music charts and music became an obsession. Whilst in school, I met Patrick Oliver. I assume it must have been on the playground because back then he was academically much better than me and our paths would never cross in a classroom. Patrick looked angelic. He had bright blue eyes, a bowl cut hair style and was very polite. He came from a good home and was well brought up by his parents, Michael and Tess. Patrick lived close to me, on Victoria Road, so we started meeting after school. We struck up a friendship, based again on football and music. It turned out that Patrick was a drummer, as well as a decent guitar player, singer and did a bit on the piano; all in all, he was a bit of a musical prodigy. Adam had also got a guitar for his birthday and had written a few songs. I was fantastic on the tambourine and could hold a tune so a band was formed. Now I use the word band very loosely as early practices involved a potato shaker, a Casio keyboard and an empty Quality Street tin for drums. Incidentally, every home seemed to have this empty tin of Quality Street back then, that would never actually contain any sweets; instead, they would all be replaced by sewing equipment. All songs were written by ourselves and because of that, we were going to rule the world. We'd decided on the name Ectoplasm. This was chosen after great debate, namely, by getting a dictionary and literally pointing at a random word. We didn't realize at the time, but Ectoplasm was the residue from unearthly spirits in the 80s hit movie, Ghostbusters. As with all bands, we were not just mates, we were a gang. We had recruited new members Ritchie Care, Keiran James, Jonathan Kibble, and James McCusker, who, in turn, added groupies, Ross Hayes, Johnathan Fellows and a boy nicknamed Plug. He was given this name due to his resemblance of a character from the children's comic, The Beano. Ritchie was a fantastic musician, and our lead guitarist, always coming up with an infectious riff. To this day I am amazed Ritchie never went further in music business. Keiran lived next door to Adam, I'm fairly sure he hadn't seen a bass guitar before joining the band, let alone played one. But, as we were missing a bass player, he seemed to fit the bill. James McCusker was brought in on keyboard, although I never actually remember him being there. Jonathan Kibble was our part time, stand in guitarist.

In 1996, England, again, had just been eliminated at the semi final stage, this time at Euro 96 and again, by Germany on penalties. Oasis was about to play to the biggest audience Britain had ever seen at Knebworth. Over a quarter of a million people packed in to see the shows and amazingly one in twenty Briton's actually applied for concert tickets, this coming off the back of the success of the album '(What's the Story) Morning Glory?' This would turn out to be Britpop's crowning glory but still the country was gripped by euphoria as 'Cool Britannia' took hold. My nights were spent roaming the streets of Port Talbot, testing our bravery by going down dark lanes in the notorious 'white city' region of the town. Looking back at our behaviour, I am surprised nobody was ever convicted of a serious crime (well, one of the boys later would be, but that's another story altogether). One night, whilst playing bobby-door knocking, Jonathan decided to throw a wheelie bin over a wall. Unfortunately, a women known to us as 'Danka' was hanging her washing out at the same time. Legend had it that she had murdered her husband back in her native Bulgaria (or some other eastern European country) and was over here on the run. The wheelie bin supposedly hit her and broke her leg but this was never confirmed. If we were not down the beach sitting on the breakwater or sat down the leisure centre, warming ourselves by the hot air vents then we were out causing trouble. There was no end of potential victims and another, given a fabricated name would be 'Mike the Psyche.' A favourite trick we kept for him was to fill a milk bottle with stones, and throw it onto the roof. Inevitably, it would smash and the stones would roll down the tiles, onto the floor below, hitting Mike as he came out to investigate. Mike actually lived directly behind my parent's house so it's a wonder I was never caught. Once Mike had been visited it was on to see Dopey Cliff. The trick with Cliff was to knock on his door three or four times and run away so he got really angry. So angry, in fact, that Cliff was known to come around the side entrance brandishing a pellet gun and fire wildly at anybody unfortunate enough to still be in the vicinity. Due to my athletic training I was always 100 metres away by that time. The evening's entertainment usually ended with 'Catman.' The imaginatively titled Catman had been bestowed this nickname after vicious rumours about local residents and their missing felines. It was thought he killed the poor kitties and disposed of them in his garden. Again, this was never proved. Around the same time, it was reported that a local takeaway was also thought to be serving cat meat; maybe the two were in collaboration?

One evening, whilst attempting and failing to gain entry to a blue light disco (a blue light disco was an event for under 16 year olds, arranged by local police, to ironically prevent kids walking the streets, causing trouble). For the record, we attempted to gain entry as we were of a similar age and not being predatory. We wandered along the back streets, coming across an abandoned home whose doors had been boarded up and as kids do, we had to investigate. With military precision we planned a full raid on this home, dressed head to toe in black and even equipped ourselves with weapons, namely a table spoon. We pulled back the wooden boarding to gain entry and were amazed to find the house was still fully furnished. It had obviously been neglected for some time but for young boys, this old house was a treasure trove. We proceeded to rummage through the abandoned house. Amongst things taken were a camera, letters, binoculars and a large holdall found upstairs in a cupboard. The camera film was later developed and showed an elderly man enjoying a day out at a cricket match. Looking back, it seems sad this man's possessions and happy memories had been completely discarded as he must have had no immediate family. We ourselves were merely children back then; we had no bad intentions or certainly no malicious intent. With our loot we headed for the abandoned gas works to see what items we had recovered. We were amazed to find designer tops, still in the protective wrappings. Also found was a strange looking object. It was a small curved bar with little weights either end. Nobody could work it out. We later found out it was a 'willy weight' essentially, you put the curved end on your penis and proceeded to attempt to lift the weight, in order to strengthen the erection. We gave this sought after item to Keiran for Christmas. The item was lovingly wrapped up and placed under the family Christmas tree while no one was looking. Keiran had some job explaining what it was when he opened his gift on Christmas morning with his parents. I wonder if he still uses it. After finding so many useful items, the decision was made to return to the house to see if anything else had been left. The following night, we returned. The wooden boarding was still ajar. We entered, with Jonathan in front, again, armed with his table spoon.

As we approached the stairs, Jonathan screamed that he had seen a person at the top of landing. We were certainly not going to check if he was bluffing or not, so, again, we ran for our lives but not before, for some extraordinary reason, Jonathan decided to start a fire in the property and had it not been for Patrick putting it out, I hate to think what might have happened. Surveillance was later put on the house to determine if Jonathan had actually seen a person at the top of those stairs. It is thought a local homeless man, who was later found dead in the River Afan had been sheltering there. Over the course of two years, nights out were getting wilder with windows smashed and roads blocked. We would rip the panels from a fence down the beach front that surrounded the old whale park and place them on the bend of the road so oncoming cars could not see the hazard ahead. With regards to the smashing of windows, I can confirm that we had no idea that those offices were still being used as a scientific lab, and had we known this information at the time, we might have thought twice before doing it, just maybe mind. That particular night, we were actually stopped by the police as we walked home. A neighbour had reported the incident after hearing the sound of breaking glass. Luckily for us, we were street wise. We innocently informed the officers that we were returning home from visiting relatives, all eight of us, though we had seen two brothers, who were known to the police, franticly running away from close to where the act of vandalism took place. They fell for it; the police even thanked us before quickly leaving in search of the brothers. You may think that we got away with murder but it was not always the case.

I was unfortunate enough to be arrested one evening. I had attempted to call my dad from a phone box, which was situated at the far end of the beach, directly opposite the old JB's Nightclub. I had been to the nightclubs under sixteens disco with Adam. It certainly wasn't to our taste but it was winter and freezing outside, so we braved the appalling music. I always remember the last song to be played would be Celine Dion's song from the film, Titanic, 'My Heart Will Go On.' Young couples would smooch on the dancefloor and if you were single, it was last chance saloon to find a partner. Adam and I would always be the wallflowers though, as we considered ourselves far to cool to get involved in anything like that. The disco ended and the majority of the kids were picked up by parents waiting outside. I walked across to the phone box to call my dad, no mobile phones in those days. Using my last twenty pence, I dialled the number but only got a dead tone; the machine did not work, yet it took my money, the bastard. Now, Looking back, I should have just walked away, it was only twenty pence and I only lived a short distance away and didn't really need a lift. Instead, I picked up a rock and hurled it at the phone kiosk, completely shattering it. Feeling a sense of achievement at my gained revenge, I began my walk home when a car suddenly pulled up and I was bundled into the back of it by two men. They would later introduce themselves in the car as CID or plain clothed police. Adam, however, who was with me at the time, did not realize this and ran frantically home to telephone my parents that I had been kidnapped. I was taken to the local police station and put in a cell. Funnily enough, my parents would ring the police station to report my apparent abduction. Thankfully for them, they were informed that I was safe and sound, well, until my parents got hold of me. The police looked after me extremely well that night. I was given tea and toast and even had a TV put nearby so I could watch the friendly football international between England and Chile, if you are interested, Chile won the game two nil, Marcelo Salas scoring both goals. It's amazing what sticks in the mind. After my arrest and subsequent release under caution, it was time for a few quiet nights; it was usually with Adam, or Patrick. We'd established a routine of walking to the local shop, Spar, and no matter what the weather, we would wear matching Adidas tracksuits.

With only a pound in our pockets, we were able to buy American cola and onion rings, or even go to the Sandown Road chip shop for a chip butty. We would then proceed to sit in the newly built Afan Lido Football Club main stand to shelter from the inevitable bad weather. One particular night, for no apparent reason, we decided to get naked and run repeatedly from one side of the pitch to the other, as boys do. We even stood in the centre circle mooning those in the club. Mooning means, bending over to show your bare arse cheeks. I think we secretly hoped that those in the clubhouse behind the goal would actually see us, they never did. I wish CCTV would have been more prominent in those days. That would have been some viewing.

In 1997, I was fortunate to get tickets to see my childhood heroes, Oasis. As it was such a momentous occasion in my life, I can actually remember the exact date, twenty years later. It was December 10th 1997, at the Cardiff International Arena. Oasis was undeniably the biggest group in the world back then. Their third album 'Be Here Now' had recently become the biggest selling album, based on first day sales, of all time. I literally counted down the days to see my idols. The concert itself will go down as one of the greatest days of my life. As usual back then, I was accompanied by Adam, and also my brothers Mike and John. Mike and John headed to the bar, while Adam and I made our way down the front to be close to the stage as possible. We managed to reach the barriers, right in front the stage. The warm up band that evening were an up and coming Scottish band called Travis. I thought they were fantastic. We waited with anticipation for the main event and we didn't have to wait long. The lights went down and the Thin Lizzy song, 'The Boys Are Back in Town' started to play. The arena erupted. The band emerged from a giant telephone box to raucous noise. I think Adam and me failed to appreciate the enormity of the concert, as we soon began to feel crushed by the forward movement of people from the back. The opening song began to play but rather than concentrate on our idols, who were now inches from us, our priorities were to get as far away from the barrier as possible. As luck would have it, we pushed through a sea of nine thousand bodies and somehow bumped right into my brothers. From there we were able to enjoy the rest of the concert. It was an unforgettable experience, seeing a band at the height of their powers. I have seen the band several times since and nothing will ever live up to that night.

In Late 1997, the trend of seeing new things for the first time would continue as Adam Cardy, Patrick Oliver and myself were taking a leisurely stroll along the promenade of Aberavon Beach. Today, the area is a new build housing estate, but back then, it was just sand dunes that stretched as far as the docks. We walked along, minding our own business, when we were surprised to discover a photographer and what we now know to be his model, hiding away in a large dune. It was obviously a photo shoot for a porn magazine. The young lady had no clothing on. So as most young boys would do in the same situation, we watched, while crouching down as not to be seen. We maneuvered to get a better view and I'm pleased to say we saw the whole thing, quite literally. The young lady took up some very seductive looking poses and I'm sure the resulting pictures were of some note, as were the memories for three impressionable young boys.

Chapter Three

'Another turning point...'

The highlight of the summer of 1997 was the anticipation of our upcoming holiday. Adam and I went to Tenerife along with my parents. With our matching clothes, Adidas Sambas and by now, matching Oasis hair do's we were ready to go. We thought we looked the bollocks and I can confirm, 19 years on, we actually did! The first few days were as normal as you would expect for a 14 year old on holiday, days by the pool and nights sat with the parents playing bingo or watching some god awful tribute act. That would change during the third day, not just the holiday, but life changing. Whilst walking along the prom, we came across a bar called, of all things, Oasis. Such was our love of the band, we assumed it must have some connection. Safe to say that it didn't, it was a Hawaiian theme bar. Nonetheless, after some persuading, my parents agreed to let us go on the condition we didn't drink alcohol. I promise that we went in with best of intentions to stick to my parents orders, however, sometimes; things are out of our control. Upon reaching the bar, we were greeted by a gentleman who we later would know as 'Hodge'. Two Coca Colas were requested and then came the immortal words: "Coke? Coke? We don't sell coke! You will have a beer!" Obviously shaken by his demands and not wanting to offend our host, we reluctantly agreed. Beer, however, was not to my young mouths taste, so beer was substituted for the alcopop known as Hooch. An hour later, and some 5 bottles each, the worsening state was confirmed with Adam requesting "another Hodge please Hooch." This was further confirmed when my dad walked in, inspected the table full of bottles and inquired had we been drinking? We obviously denied these accusations, while stumbling to our feet. We were subsequently walked back to the hotel while we giggled like school girls. The rest of the night involved the room, for some unexplained reason, appearing to spin. Sadly that night, Princess Diana was killed in car crash in Paris. Adam put to bed any suspicions that he was involved by declaring, when informed of the princess' demise the next morning, "I didn't do it."

The remaining days were spent by the pool with a large group of friends we had met. There were no holiday romances of note but I did fall in love with the way Brummies' say 'cup of tea' or 'kip ov teee' as it sounded to me. I got this unfortunate girl to repeat this sentence over and over, she must have been glad when I went home. It was a wonderful coming of age trip and even cemented my lifelong friendship with Adam. One evening, we got into a fight after Adam had almost been pushed backwards off the prom wall by a dark skinned boy over a misheard comment about Michael Jackson. The incident happened outside the bar my parents were in. Adam and I were sat on the wall with a group of friends we had made. The wall was level with the prom in front, but behind was at least a 20 foot drop onto the sand below. Whilst we were all chatting away, others in the group must have been having a different conversation because Adam mentioned Michael Jackson in reference to a song that was being sung on karaoke. For some reason, one of the boys took exception to that comment and shoved Adam, almost off the wall, down to the ground below. We both paused in shock, before jumping up and confronting this boy. By now his two mates had backed him up, they were considerably older than us but we weren't going to back down. A few heated words were exchanged and we ended up chasing them down the prom. We headed back to the bar to meet my parents and told them what had happened. My parents were fantastic that whole trip, allowing us that little bit of independence, though not enough for us to abuse our little bit of freedom. The same night, whilst walking to the toilet and almost as a reward for our good behaviour, we came across female strippers getting changed in a side room. They were fully aware that we were there but no made no effort to cover up and we certainly made no effort to look away. The excitement must have become all too much for Adam as once in the toilet, I ended up getting urinated on. Now, I feel I should explain that last comment. I was at the urinal, minding my own business, when I felt a warm sensation running down my leg. I glanced, curiously to my left and there was Adam, joyfully pissing on me. I assume it had something to do with alcohol? Or maybe he thought I'd been stung by a jellyfish? Either way, he was having the time of his life. Being the young man I was becoming and having supposedly learned my lesson about acting on impulse, I, of course, pissed back on him. We both slipped and ended up on the urine soaked toilet floor, again, giggling like girls. The holiday was finished off with a relaxing boat ride. Walking down to the harbour a few of the locals saw us and started shouting "Oasis" "Gallagher's." We tried our best to be them back then so this was exactly the effect we were after. It made our day. Adam lost a certain element of coolness that day after spending the majority of the trip with his head over the side of the boat being sick.

The holiday was a first coming of age experience for the both of us. We both returned with a new level of confidence. It was this new level of confidence that would lead me to another unwanted meeting with the local police. I had gone to Neath town centre with Jonathan and a boy named Woggy. We were in the town's Woolworth store, browsing albums when Woggy mentioned that if we wanted them, we could take them. He showed us how easy it was by simply putting them in his coat. I put what happened next to being easily led. Jonathan and I decided to steal one or maybe three. It could have even been four. I forget the exact figure. We removed the security stickers, placed them in our jackets and began to leave. Woggy made it safely outside with his haul but I had spotted the Radiohead album, 'The Bends.' I had wanted this album for a while so I simply stole it. Jonathan helped himself as well. We removed the security tag and put them in our jackets. We couldn't believe how easy this was. We confidently walked past the check out and began to pick up the pace as we aimed for the front door. We thought we had made it out without detection. I opened the door and was just about to step out when we were grabbed by security. Woggy ran and he was not caught. The security handed me over to the store manager. He asked the name and address of the other boy who was with me; I denied any knowledge of anybody else being involved. He showed me CCTV of me entering the store and browsing with two boys. I said it must have been a coincidence as I did not know him. Due to my refusal to co-operate and due to the value of the stolen items, the police were called for. I didn't mind dealing with the police, it was my parents I was terrified of. They had raised me to know better than that and I definitely let them down that day. I was taken to Neath Police Station, put into a cell and later interviewed. No charges were made and I was released under caution. Jonathan suffered a similar fate, although he reliably informs me that his dad gave him a sufficient hiding for the crime when he got home.

Chapter Four

'End of a century....'

Upon my return from Tenerife and on the wave of having experienced independence, my life experiences would move on to the next level. In the summer of 1998 England was knocked out of the World Cup in France, in the last 16 stage by Argentina. The game being memorable as eighteen year old Michael Owen scored a wonder goal for England. This would later be overshadowed by a David Beckham red card for a kick at Diego Simeone. England was eventually beaten on a penalty shootout again. France would go on to win the final on home soil, beating defending champions Brazil, 3-0. The 1998/99 sporting season would also prove memorable for Manchester United, as they won an unprecedented treble. Winning the Premier league and both FA Cup and Champions League. Meanwhile, closer to home, Wales' rugby team had beaten England at Wembley, with Scott Gibbs scoring an iconic late try. They followed this up with a series win out in Argentina and then defeating South Africa in the opening game at the Millennium Stadium. This proved quite a turn-around for the team as twelve months earlier, Wales had been humiliated 96-13 against the South Africans. Hopes were high heading into the Rugby World Cup later that year, which was to be held in Wales. Unfortunately there would be no fairy-tale ending as Wales were knocked out in the quarter finals by eventual winners, Australia. Rather than be despondent, the country was on a high. The euphoria of 'Cool Britannia' was to be replaced by 'Cool Cymru.' Bands such as The Stereophonics, Manic Street Preachers, Feeder, Super Furry Animals and Catatonia, topped the UK charts and actor Rhys Ifans became a household name. All were flying the Welsh flag globally and proudly. In 1999, the end of the year would herald the start of a new Millennium. Closer to home and also caught up in the Welsh pride, my friends and I were dreaming of being the next big thing to come out of the country.

I was still in the band, Ectoplasm. Practices were becoming more frequent, better songs were being written and soon, gigs were being arranged. All the boys in the band had the same haircut, namely, scruffy. We looked and acted the way up and coming rock stars should, at least we thought we did. We really started to believe that we could have a genuine career in music. We had upgraded our rehearsal room to the local scout's hall, which replaced the previous venue of Adam's bedroom.

Gone were the potato shaker and Quality Street tin for drums and things were now becoming more organised. One day after school, Patrick Oliver showed me the lyrics to a song he'd written called 'Daytona Dreaming.' The title was taken from a suggested Oasis album name which was never used. Patrick had a talent for writing catchy songs. He seemed to focus more on writing words about growing up and living your dreams, whereas Adam was writing songs about his experiences in relationships, edgy, heartfelt words. Richie was the rocker of the band and his guitar would be the driving force behind our sound. He and Keiran had a wider range of influences other than the Britpop dominated bands we listened too. As a result, we had a style and sound of our own compared to other bands in the area. For a band made up of boys so young, we were very confident. Instead of school discos or church halls, we started playing in a local pub called the Bay View on a Sunday afternoons. It smelled of stale beer and the room always seemed to have a constant cloud of smoke, hovering at eye level. It's the kind of room you will never see again because of the smoking ban. It had the same faces, singing the same songs, every Sunday. It was brilliant! Our first main gig came on a Friday night supporting one of the bands from the Bay View called Backtrax. The gig was in the Jersey Beach

Hotel, a grand looking place which stood on the corner of the road down on Aberavon beach front. As seems to have happened to a lot of the old pubs in Port Talbot, including the Bay View, it mysteriously burned down a few years back. In fact, the majority of the venues we played in subsequently burned down. Strange that! The gig itself took place on a busy Friday night so the bar was packed with people. We all had a few drinks to calm the nerves, and then it was time for our big moment. We were allowed to play our own songs which seemed to go down quite well. It's a fantastic feeling to play to a crowd, and although not everyone was watching us, we were well received by most. At the end of the gig, people even came up to us and ask us what bands songs we had played. They seemed impressed when we told them that we had written them ourselves. This would be our problem; people looked at us and judged us on our age. They were pleasantly surprised once they heard us play but getting heard in the first place was turning out to be harder than it looked. Payment for our performance that night consisted of chicken and chips in a basket and flavoured vodka. They deemed this suitable for a band made up of 15 year olds, though obviously, we never complained. After the gig we walked home triumphantly. No matter what happened from now on, we would always have that night to look back on and be proud our efforts. Patrick Oliver stayed over at my house that night, we wrote a song, fantastically titled, 'Cast a Cold Eye.' The lyrics from the song would go on to become the title of this book. The words, cast a cold eye, we later found out, were taken from the Irish poet, William Butler Yeats work, named, Under Ben Bulben. The words are also etched onto the gravestone of the writer. I still to this day have no idea where either of us would have come into contact with the works of Yeats, though I feel an appropriate mention was required. A few days after our first performance in the Jersey Beach Hotel, we had our very own gig in the Red Dragon pub, down in the Sandfields estate. In our minds we were the best band in the area. We had no evidence to back this up except we knew nobody would have the same spirit that we had. This was our dream and we'd spend hours, days, together, rehearsing down the scout's hall but not just as band but also as friends. We turned up to the pub and instead of being greeted by hundreds of fans or swamped by female groupies, we were met by an old man in a flat cap, drinking a pint of bitter, eating a pie, while watching the six o'clock news. We knew we had to start somewhere; we wouldn't be stars overnight so we set up and began our performance as normal. We opened with a song titled, 'Oxymoron.' We had even rehearsed an introduction; the band would walk on stage, one by one, each member would pretend to tune the guitars, or fiddle with the drums before the song begun. Once, everyone was on stage, the opening chords would play. I would walk on shaking my tambourine, before letting out an almighty scream as the song kicked in. Maybe this introduction might have been more suited to the arenas and stadiums we imagined ourselves in, as upon my scream, the old man sat at the table got up as if to walk out but instead walked over to the plug and unplugged the amplifiers, before shuffling back to his seat, muffling some profanity towards us and continuing his pint. Funnily enough, we never saw the old man who we nicknamed, Pies, at any of our future gigs. I was now at an age where I was faced with a crossroads. As much as I enjoyed being part of a band, I was also part of a team elsewhere. I was a talented rugby player and I soon encountered a dilemma. I had to make a decision on which of my dreams I wanted to commit to. Sundays at the Bay View were still going ahead but mainly without me. Other, more prominent gigs were being arranged but due to my rugby career, the band was being neglected on my part. I missed practices and I even missed a demo recording. This behaviour wasn't fair to my mates and I subsequently left, much to my regret. Patrick Oliver would also leave the group a few years later. Without mention to his friends, he left his home and moved up to the North East via Manchester, where he has stayed to this day. This caused friction between Adam and Patrick, who didn't speak for years after. Thankfully, they are now on speaking terms. By the end of 1999, my dreams of being a rock star were diminishing but my hopes of being a successful rugby player were looking promising.

As I mentioned earlier, as a result of being a suspected problem child, I was ushered into rugby and as I also mentioned, it seemed to come naturally to me. I was fortunate that my dad spent hours training me. I was now a teenager, but I was advanced beyond my years with my father mentoring me. He was my biggest fan and also my biggest critic. He would praise me if I had played well but would also highlight areas in which I could improve on. Together, we spent nights running down the beach, hill sprints and tackling on the sand. My brother even gave me a weights programme. I loved it. This training certainly helped my overall athletic performance as I entered, and won the Welsh Boys Clubs, West Wales, athletic event in the 100 metres and 800 metres. I was invited for the national trials to be held in Cardiff. I lined up at the start and glanced around at the other sprinters. They all had starting blocks and running spikes, I had my normal running trainers and began from a standing position. Nevertheless, I did quite well, finishing 4th in both races despite having very little race experience. For some unknown reason, I was still continuously overlooked for the school athletic teams, despite easily winning the West Wales Championships. I put it down to the teachers seeing me as a problem child. Those were days together with my dad that helped me develop. I don't give my dad enough credit for the influence he has had on me and looking back now, I think I took for granted just how many hours he put into helping me achieve my goal. My dad would work all day carrying out physical labour and then come home in time to take me training for a few hours. I also look back on the invaluable advice he gave me, advice I probably didn't take at the time but wish I did. If I can be half the father he was then I will be happy. The same applies to my mother, although not as hands on as my dad, my mother was always encouraging me, making me believe in myself. I'd spent my entire junior career at the Aberavon Green Stars. The team consisted mainly of players from the school, St Josephs, which I attended. Our rivals were Aberavon Quins, who were mainly made up of boys from the Fairfield area of town. During one of these heated derbies, myself and Matthew Rowlands were sent off for fighting though not a single punch was thrown. We both stood there, taking it turns to kick each other in the shins. It's amazing that even at that young age you can get caught up in the emotion of a big game and be willing to do anything to win. By 1999, a break-away team was formed, made up of the best players in Port Talbot. I almost never made it this far in my rugby career as in 1998 I had a brief spell away from the game. I had become increasingly swayed by the band and also at the time, my football career. I played for Afan Lido, a well-known team, who, at the time, played in the Welsh Premiership. We had some decent local players and good coaches in Tony Davies and Michael Cooling. I had formed a good strike partnership with Damian Adams. As I mentioned earlier, I'd known Damian from a young age, we walked to school together every morning. He would come over to play computer games or we would go for a kick about down the park a couple of times a week. He also stayed at Butlin's with me and my parents. We seemed to be on the same wave length on the football pitch, we ought to have done, the amount of hours we'd spent playing in that park together. We even had a ritual of swapping one boot each, I had green boots, Damian had yellow boots, and we would swap one each to match the team kit. One season, we won the treble, undefeated in winning the league and two cups.

Between us we must have scored sixty goals. Damian was a fantastic footballer and fitted the criteria perfectly for the maverick that he was. Energetic, unpredictable, wicked, but all with a great sense of humour and always with a smile on his face. As with most childhood friendships, as you get older you lose touch with people who were once close to you. Sadly, Damian must have hidden his demons well behind his smile, as he took his own life in 2015. This would be the second tragedy to hit the family, as Damien's younger brother, Dominik, had also taken his own life a few years earlier on exactly the same stretch of the train track. I knew both boys very well, and struggle to comprehend what could drive two, young, outgoing boys to commit such an act. As with all deaths in this way, it would be too late to tell them just how well thought of they were. The hurt was intensified as a day after being made aware of Damian's death I noticed I had received a friend request from his new account on Facebook. Maybe this was a cry for help? I'll never know. Either way, I will always have great memories of a great childhood friend.

(Below) Damian

Chapter Five

'Different gear, still speeding...'

After a brief exodus from the game and after deciding that I didn't have the required skills to be the next Diego Maradona, I dedicated myself to rugby. I joined the new team who would be based down at Taibach RFC. I knew most of the players having either played with them, or against them. We had a good, experienced coaching team of Tony Staton, Phil Terry, Phil Jenkins and Steve Gadd, all of whom which played at various levels of the Welsh leagues. Their advice was invaluable. The following four seasons are easily my favourite on a rugby pitch and off it. We were lucky to play for a great club who looked after us and with some good experienced senior players always ready to take you under their wing, usually at the bar after the game. As well as being memorable on the pitch, it was equally memorable off the pitch, with some fantastic end of season tours to look back on. During a trip to Blackpool, we arranged a match against a county team from England, East Sussex. To highlight the quality we had in the team, a senior member of the opposition approached us to ask us to take the game more seriously as apparently we were messing about during the warm ups. The night before we had all been out until the early hours so we were in good spirits. Our coach, Tony, informed us of the gentleman's request, and instructed us to not take it easy on them. We ended up winning the game 69-7. The highlight of the tour was Leon Cronin stripping naked and proceeding to streak during a cricket match that was taking place. As if this was not bad enough, he went even further by rugby tackling the poor umpire, leaving him flat out on the floor and apparently breaking a few of his ribs. The second end of season tour was to Newcastle. Within hours of being there, Michael McSweeney had been body slammed like a wrestler through a glass table at the hotel bar by a player who shall remain nameless, but did go on to represent his country and also the coach, Phil Jenkins, having an ice bucket full of water poured over his head while we waited to go out for the night, again, by the same player who shall remain nameless. Phil didn't see the funny side and chased the nameless offender to his hotel room. There was an angry exchange of words and a brief scuffle ensued, resulting in both men clattering into a TV stand. Luckily, I managed to catch the television before it hit the ground. As usual, this team didn't do just normal behaviour. The following day, we travelled to play Ryton Rugby Club. The game itself was not notable for the standard of play but was memorable for Richard Hibbard and myself getting sin binned at the same time. We made our way to the touch line but were ordered by the referee to stand separately at either end of the pitch and directly behind the goal posts. The bizarre instruction was followed up by the referee telling us not to watch the game and to face away from the pitch and to keep it that way until it was time to come back on. We had to stand there for ten minutes watching the traffic passing by. The team spirit at this club was like nothing I have ever experienced since, from the players, to the coaches, the committee men, the bar staff the whole club was like a big family. The team was arguably the finest youth team to come out of Port Talbot. The back row itself contained four Welsh youth internationals in, myself, Richard Hibbard, Michael Kelly and Tom Smith. Many other players in the team could or should have gone on to greater things. Success on the pitch came too easy to us at local level, winning leagues, cups, 7's and 10's tournaments. No fewer than twelve players received a recognised Welsh cap over the three seasons. Looking back, the seven-a-side tournament team had a vast array of talent. The forwards were myself, Hibbard, Mike Kelly or Tom Smith with Mike Sweeney, Kyle Jenkins, Mark Fender, and either Ashley Davies Richard Lewis or Matthew Rowlands in the back line. We hammered everybody. We didn't even have to really try. We also beat an up and coming Aberavon Quins team in the final of the ten-a-side tournament. They performed exceptionally well on the day and it highlighted the talent being produced in our town at the time. As mentioned, we had great success in the local youth league. In our first season as sixteen year olds, we finished second in the league playing against teams two years our senior, who were often physically more developed than we were. We would have won the title on the last game of the season too, had I not missed with a penalty from the halfway line against Tonmawr. This should have come as a warning to other clubs as the following year we won every trophy on offer, remaining undefeated in the process. I also had the honour of finishing joint top try scorer with winger, Mark Fender, both scoring twenty six tries, in only eighteen games. We were promoted to the Welsh Youth Premier League and had it not been for international call-ups, I'm sure we would have won that as well. The eventual winners were a very good Cross Keys team who beat us home and away. Frustratingly, we also lost in two cup semi-finals in that final season, defeated by local rivals Skewen and Resolven. I think we were under the impression that all we had to do was turn up for the win. Realistically, we should have had too much skill and power for both teams but both Skewen and Resolven were up for the fight and deserved their victories over us. This has to be up there as one of the biggest disappointments and regrets of my career. The stage had been set for our final hurrah. We had been together, not just as teammates but also as lifelong friends. We knew these would more than likely, be our final games together as a team and we blew it. The grand ending turned into nothing more than a damp squib. The team was disbanded shortly after, with some players going on to semi-professional clubs, while others remained at Taibach but moved up to senior rugby. As with most clubs, there were groups of friends within the team. My group, made up of James Jones, Richard Hibbard, Andrew Gadd, Andrew Redmore, Craig 'Midgie' Clements and Matthew Noble, preferred to visit the local pubs, whereas the other group in the team would venture to Swansea for the nightclubs. We also had a Wednesday night routine of visiting the cinema, or the Aquadome, the local swimming baths in Port Talbot. It had fantastic slides, a wave machine and a large Jacuzzi which we all took advantage of. It must also be the only swimming bath's in history to burn down but that it did in 2009. As mentioned earlier, Port Talbot seems to have a bizarre history of well-known landmarks appearing to almost spontaneously combust before the land is inevitably and conveniently sold to the local council, usually for housing purposes. Shortly after leaving school, I went to Benidorm with Andrew Redmore and a few others to celebrate our GCSE results. I left school with no real qualifications to speak of but I liked the idea of the going away. My only real memory of the holiday is being threatened with deportation from Spain over damage caused to a lift. We had been on a Club 18-30 event and free sangria was provided. I vaguely remember a bar crawl and the rest is a mystery. It is thought, in my drunken state that I punched the glass panel to the lift, rendering it beyond repair. A member of staff spotted the damage and subsequently followed the trail of blood which led straight to my room. I had no alibi. One of the boys also decided to steal the picture that hung from the hotel room wall as a souvenir for their mother. The manager was furious over the damages and demanded cash. We had nothing left between us so the police were called. It was suggested that we be sent back to the UK but as it was our last day, we were going home anyway. The police waited to make sure we got on the bus to go to the airport and we left Benidorm, thankfully, not in handcuffs.

After a rugby match on a Saturday, the ritual involved meeting at a designated house, usually my parents, bringing any alcohol you could find, usually vodka, wine, whisky, rum, brandy, which was poured into a bowl to create the most horrific tasting punch you could imagine. This was then topped off with fruit juice to hopefully hide the taste. Then it was onto our local town. Port Talbot town centre was a rough place back then. You could guarantee scenes resembling the Wild West come throwing out time. Station Road is where boys become men. Most of the pubs would be full with men who were local rugby players or hardened steel workers, or even worse, both. You could sense the testosterone just walking in the pub. The street in question had maybe ten pubs on a fifty metre road. There were also two kebab shops, a small taxi rank, an Indian restaurant and at the far end, a small police station to maintain order. Next to the police station was a nightclub named, The Apollo. This is where most night's recollections would end for me. The club itself was a sweat box, quite literally. There was obviously no crowd management as it was dangerously overcrowded and the heat off those crammed in would cause the moisture to rise to the ceiling before dripping on those dancing below. I personally hated it because the heat made my, then, perfectly styled hair, frizzy. It wasn't unusual back then to wake up the next morning with a half-eaten kebab, pizza or even the occasional broken wrist. I actually missed most of a cup final as a result of one of these nights out. I foolishly attempted to flag a taxi down by stepping into its path. Not a good idea! The taxi hit me, spun me around and I landed on the kerb, arse first. The bruising was most impressive; however, I didn't recover in time and only made the bench in Taibach's defeat to Aberavon. My misery was compounded when I was sin binned after only thirty seconds after coming on. I would later go onto beat this impressive record.

Chapter Six

'Well we used to be the best of friends and we used to hang around...'

It was at Taibach that I first met another good friend, Richard Hibbard. I was aware of who he was after playing junior rugby against him. He stood out even then, with a big build and blonde curtained hairstyle. I saw him regularly as his family home was opposite my comprehensive school. He was always with his dog, Watson; a beautiful golden retriever. They looked quite similar in those days. I was later told a funny story about the Statue of St Joseph in the school grounds. Often as a child, I'd walk into school and notice our mascot was missing a particular part of its body. It later transpired that Hibbard's brothers, Nick and Daniel, who were both a few years older than Richard, owned an air rifle. The sight of the statue directly opposite the family house could not be resisted and the head was shot off on multiple occasions. Even back then, Hibbard was an imposing person, especially after a few whiskies. We got on from the start, I think because at the time, we were the only players with an interest in the gym. It also soon turned out we were both, mildly putting it, mad bastards. If anything happened, it would more often than not be us responsible for it. We were once sent back to the hotel whilst on tour in Newcastle. We had gone bowling as a team to the Metro Centre. As we were about to play, a committee man approached us and said he had received a phone call from the hotel and that we had to return immediately to clean our room, as the staff had refused to do it. Our crime? We had, for some reason in a drunken state, shaved our pubes off in the sink and left them there. Obviously there were certain elements of our behaviour that confirmed we were out of control but personally, I think we just played up to our reputation. At the same time, we both seemed the only ones fully focused before games. The night before the match, we'd eat right, discuss team moves and most importantly, not get pissed. Pre-season we would often train alone, pulling a large tyre around the field or running up mountains being chased by sheep. Even going to away games we would usually isolate ourselves away from the other players who'd be laughing and joking at the back, while we sat at the front of the team bus. On tour, we'd take the game the next day seriously and not drink. On the trip to Blackpool, instead of going out with the team the day before the game, we went to Blackpool Tower and did a bit of shopping and sightseeing. We'd obviously make up for the previous days restraint by drinking after the match. Besides our professional approach to the game, we were labelled liabilities, sometimes, correctly.

One night, I was leaving the St Oswald's pub in Port Talbot to go home. When I got outside, I realised that Hibbard was due to stay in my parents' house. I tapped the window and calmly mouthed "I'm off" to which Hibbard stood up and angrily punched the whole window through shouting "don't tell me to fuck off." I shook my head and informed him through the large hole where the glass once was, that I merely said "I'm off," NOT, "fuck off." He just replied innocently, "oh sorry." Even more amazing was how he convinced the door staff that somebody from outside had actually smashed the window, even though the glass was outside on the road. Obviously the force would have had come from inside the premises. By now, his hand was also bleeding badly. Somehow, he got out of there without being arrested and he spent the rest of the night on my bedroom floor, still bleeding badly. As with most of my friendships back then, alcohol seemed to play a major part. I'm not sure if that's a good thing or a bad thing but it makes for some interesting stories.

As with most boisterous teenagers, messing around comes naturally. It was during this messing around that Hibbard and I had a play fight that got quite serious. Somehow, I ended up breaking my wrist so we travelled to the accident and emergency room in Morrison Hospital, Swansea. We were both still pissed, and pissed off at each other, not a word had been said, so when Hibbard got up to go outside, I assumed he was going home. I couldn't blame him, it was silly o'clock in the morning, freezing cold and had began to snow. An hour had had passed when a woman came into the waiting room, concern over her face, asking if anybody knew the young boy asleep on the bench outside. She also added that the boy appeared to be turning blue. Intuition told me to look, and there was Richard, fast asleep on the bench with about a foot of snow on him. He was, indeed, turning blue. I left him there while I was put in a cast for my broken wrist and then booked us a taxi home. Hibbard spent the entire journey with his head resting on the unfortunate drivers shoulder, dribbling. This was a fairly standard night back then. During a tour to Butlin's in Minehead, Hibbard had fallen asleep, so, as young boys will, we decided to shave his eyebrows off. The search for a razor turned out to be unsuccessful. Disappointment gripped the chalet then, someone had a brainwave. He walked out of the room briefly but soon returned with, of all things, a cheese grater. I can confirm that a cheese grater is not a suitable replacement for a shaving device and it's a wonder the scarring was not permanent. Hibbard was not always the victim. One morning, in the hotel bedroom, whilst on tour to Newcastle, a play fight broke out between Hibbard and our unfortunate roommate Matthew Noble. I say unfortunate because nobody wanted to share a room with us two. I've no idea why. Back to the play fight, and aware of my previous injuries in these situations, I decided to keep a safe distance. Both men wrestled on the ground, with Noble eventually getting the upper hand. Hibbard felt behind him on the bedside cabinet for a suitable weapon to fend Noble off. I watched as his searching hand felt a plastic water bottle and a hair brush. He dismissed both items. He finally settled for the ceramic table lamp, which he proceeded to whack Noble over the head with. A smash and fused circuit board later, the fight was over. Noble was left groaning on the floor, wondering what he had done so that his punishment was to be put in a room with the two of us. There are quite a few more stories involving tours and other nights out which I can't go into, probably for legal reasons.

Besides the wild nights, Hibbard was also a good friend, we were inseparable for years. We were also notorious for posing up town in the tightest clothes we owned. This seems to be the legacy of those days, which still gets mentioned, as do our appearances in the annual Taibach Christmas pantomime. The Pantomime takes an adult spin on well-known plays. It is an entirely amateur production, made up of players and committee men from the rugby club. The script is even written by club stalwarts Mark Miles, Colin Deere and directed by Aled Humphreys. Part of the legendary show is the famous strip scene. I still very much doubt the balloon dance routine in which Hibbard and I were actually fully naked, full frontal, will ever be forgotten for those lucky enough to be in attendance, especially in the front row. For all the crazy stories, Hibbard has done fantastically well for himself since those days. He has had a fantastic career with the Ospreys, and He is still making the headlines, across the border with Gloucester. His greatest success would have to be internationally, representing Wales on no fewer than thirty eight occasions, scoring two tries, and winning the 2013 six nations title in the process. Richard also had the honour of being selected for the British and Irish

Lions on their winning tour of Australia in 2013. Hibbard is now happily married to Louise and they have three beautiful children. His Mam, Syriol, who was a wonderful woman, is sadly no longer with us but would be immensely proud, as am I.

Hibbard and Me after the Taibach panto

(Above) Me and Hibbard. Taibach youth rugby tour. 2000

(Below) Traditional Sunday morning at my mams

Chapter Seven

'Looks like we made it....'

On September 11th 2001, the world was rocked by a terror attack on the World Trade Centre in New York. I had just been signed by Swansea Rugby Club, along with Richard Hibbard. We started out by playing for the clubs' under 19's team on a Wednesday, whilst still playing for Taibach Youth on the weekend. The step in class was obvious. We were playing against other top class players and playing on well-known grounds such as Cardiff Arms Park, Rodney Parade in Newport and the Rec, home of Bath. Such was the competitive nature that one game against Pontypridd, on a particularly wet and windy night, actually finished 0-0. To this day, I do not know of any other game of rugby to finish with this score line. I was fortunate enough to be selected for Wales and played in the successful Home Nation's tournament, held in Leeds, against Ireland, Scotland (on my 18th birthday) and England. Training for an international tournament was brutal.

We attended a training weekend at the RAF base in St Athan, near Cardiff. It took place just three days before Christmas but there were no festive niceties involved here. On the very first night, we had to complete a bleep test. The expectations were astounding. One of my club team mates, Mike Kelly, outperformed everyone to reach a fantastically high score. After that, it was body fat testing. If anyone failed to reach the expected levels by the given time, then they would be out of the squad. The remaining few days was spent running 200 metre sprints, every twenty seconds for twenty repetitions. It was a killer. The day began at six in the morning until bed and lights out at nine at night. It was like a military camp. The pressure was enormous; you could no longer rely on ability alone, you had to know and understand team moves, line out calls as well as individual goals. Standards were set that you couldn't drop below, if you did, you were out. It was a great experience and nothing will beat the pride of playing for your country, especially as the anthems are sung. The call-up's continued as I was selected for the Welsh Crawshays and Welsh President's teams. It seemed I had made a name for myself. Sadly, not long after, my Nan passed away. A few days before, I had gone to the nursing home where she was, in my full welsh suit and also took my Welsh cap. She didn't say due to her illness, but I know she would have been proud. At the age of eighteen, I had also been selected for Swansea's first team against Pontypridd, who had legendary Wales outside half Neil Jenkins playing that night. It was a bizarre story as both Hibbard and I had received a call about playing that evening. We both assumed it was the club's under 21's team. We were picked up by the coach and were amazed to find it was actually the full first team, with a number of current Welsh internationals that we would be representing. It was quite a baptism of fire that evening. Although it felt fantastic to experience the quality of professional rugby, it was also an eye opener of how much I had to develop, both mentally and physically. The season ended well for me as I also made appearances against Newport and Llanelli, both televised and both against teams full of well-known international players. The game against Llanelli was a high scoring game, finishing 40-33 to Swansea. A young Mike Phillips scored a hat trick for the visitors that evening. Before the game, the coach had highlighted Mike Phillips as a weakness. The Wales scrum half at the time, Dwayne Peel was supposed to start the game but pulled out due to injury. The coach instructed us to run at Mike Phillips and intimidate this young boy. Turns out this young boy was six foot three and sixteen stone and in time, would prove that he liked the physical side of the game. Mike Phillips went on to become Wales' most capped scrum-half, overtaking, ironically, the man he replaced that night, Dwayne Peel. The game against Newport will be remembered for two incidents. The first was South African, World Cup winning full back, Percy Montgomery being sent off for pushing the touch judge to the ground and the second was this being the last ever game that Swansea RFC would play as a stand-alone professional club before merging with Neath to form the Ospreys. The game was another high scoring end of season match, finishing 44-33 to Swansea. The referee that night would later go on to officiate in the World Cup final and be considered the finest referee in the world, Nigel Owens. At the end of the game, I managed to get myself some memorabilia of this historic night by acquiring club legend, Scott Gibbs' match shirt and shorts. It felt surreal being in the changing room or sharing a pitch with players you were watching in awe just twelve months ago. I didn't feel overwhelmed, it was all happening so fast that I don't think I realised the enormity of what was going on. As I left the ground, supporters were waiting in the car park to meet the players. A young boy come over and asked me for my autograph. My initial reaction was 'Me? You want my autograph?' I was still contemplating whether I should ask Scott Gibbs for his autograph and he was on my team.

Now I had a small boy wanting mine, it was a nice feeling. I, of course, agreed but as I was so new to this that I didn't even have a signature. I just wrote my name in a child-like way. I couldn't even do cursive writing, I still can't. I had enjoyed the game time. I thought I acquitted myself well for someone so young and at the time I thought I had reached my goal of playing professional rugby, being coached by some of the most respected coaches at that time and training with established international players such as Scott Gibbs, Colin Charvis and Mark Taylor. I should have developed, learnt from them, instead I thought I knew it all and failed to listen to advice. And although I am still proud of my achievements in these games, I still look back on this time as a wasted opportunity. At the end of the season, I sat down with coaches Tony Clement and Keith Colclough and agreed a new deal to stay at the club. The meeting was positive with advice given on how to build on my talents.

My time at Swansea came to an end after I foolishly turned up drunk to a pre- season team building session. I had been out that afternoon after attending a funeral. I assumed the team building later on in the day would be drinks in town so thought nothing of it. When I arrived at the meeting point, I was informed that the team building arranged was actually an assault course first with drinks later. The coach, ex-Wales international and British Lion, Tony Clement, refused to let me take part and sent me home. We spoke briefly the next day. He told me of his disappointment that I had been offered a senior contract, yet I chose to act unprofessionally before the start of what could be a big season for me. He acknowledged my talents but questioned my commitment. Looking back, I think he was trying to get a positive response from me but due to my naivety, I took this personally. I felt I was being forced out, though I now know that this was not the case, so I left Swansea and eventually signed for my home town club, Aberavon. Before the season started, Richard Hibbard and I were approached to play rugby league for the newly formed Aberavon Fighting Irish. The games were to be played during the off season, in summer. As an incentive we were offered jobs with the local Borough Council. We jumped at the chance and we soon found ourselves on placement, in a cemetery. Goytre cemetery is in the hills above Port Talbot, a quiet village in which a road runs right through the middle and is surrounded by mountains on either side. Our first job was to maintain the gardens, cutting back thorns and removing dead flowers from stagnant water. I think Hibbard lasted a day before transferring to the grass cutting team. I enjoyed the physical side of the job, heavy lifting and digging, it benefited me for the coming season. One afternoon, I was told to prepare a grave for a funeral the next day. As it was the middle of the afternoon, in the middle of summer, I took shelter in the now dug grave and pulled the wooden safety boards over me and began to lie down. I was just relaxing when I heard a scratching sound from above my head. With this being a cemetery and fully aware that I shared this space with multiple others nearby, my mind began to race at every possible explanation. I'd just began to tell myself that it was most probably falling soil when, again, I heard the scratching, coming from above. I stood up, moved the wooden covering and nervously peered out. There was nothing there, not a person to be seen. I was about to put it down to my imagination when I heard the scratching sound again, this time it was right behind me. I began to turn, slowly, scared of what unearthly being I might encounter. Had I disturbed someone's final resting place? I turned my head and came face to face with it. A peacock. Now, in my surprised state, I must have yelled, which startled the bird of paradise, which in turn opened up its wings to display its beautiful plumage and began to cry out. I dived back into the grave and almost wished it was a ghost. After a few minutes the peacock vanished. I sat there, bewildered as to why this exotic bird was roaming a cemetery in the sleepy Welsh village of

71

Goytre. I later found out that it had escaped from a nearby horse riding centre where they were kept. The rugby league itself was enjoyable, even though I had no idea what the rules were. Our first game was against a side known as The Bridgend Blue Bulls. We arrived at the ground and were surprised to be informed of the quality of players in the opposition. Ex-union and league internationals, Alan Bateman, John Devereux and Kevin Ellis were on the team sheet, as well as future international Lee Byrne, Lenny Woodard and Nathan Strong. We had a very young side, with myself, Hibbard and Richard Lewis all being barely eighteen and not really knowing the rules of the game. We came fantastically close to winning but eventually lost 26-21. In later seasons, Richard Hibbard would not be permitted to play rugby league as he was contracted to the Ospreys. That didn't stop him. In order to carry on playing he was imaginatively given the pseudonym, Hubert Richards. It would have worked as well, had a picture of him under that alias not appeared in the local paper.

Whilst working for the council, I drove a colleague's car home after his daughter had been taken ill and transferred to hospital. It would have meant him driving the van all the way back to the depot to collect his car and then driving all away back to the hospital, near to where we were working in the first place. This made no sense in the emergency so I told him to just go straight to the hospital and as we lived fairly close to each other, I informed him that when I finished work, I would get the car and simply drop it off at his house for him. It was a good deed that would go horribly wrong. The drive home started with no incident. As I drove through Port Talbot town centre, opposite the train station, the car in front of me seemed indecisive as to where he was going. I was yards from the traffic lights when they began to turn amber so decided to carry on through, as did the car in front, when, for some strange reason he slammed on after already passing the lights. I broke as hard as I could but I inevitably went into the back of him. Prick. I got out inspecting the damage; the front of my friend's car was wrecked. I approached the car I had hit and asked what he was playing at, or words to that effect. He apologised but said he was fine. The police were on the scene within minutes. There were no problems at first; it was just an unfortunate accident that they see on a daily basis. The policeman came over to inform me the man in the car was now complaining of neck pains, even the policeman said he was trying it on. The cars were moved out of the road and I was told to produce my licence and insurance at the station the next day. I took my documents to the station and upon inspection the women behind the desk asked if these are all I had. She went on to explain that my insurance was third party only and that I was not eligible to drive anybody else's car. I still didn't fully appreciate what she saying, I just apologised and said I didn't even realise, I was only helping out a friend in an emergency. A police officer came out and said they would have to charge me with driving with no insurance. I was devastated. I hadn't had my license long and I genuinely didn't know I couldn't drive any other vehicle. I was also charged with driving without due care and attention. This was another kick in the balls as I felt it was the knobhead in front of me who was at fault. I was told to appear in court. I couldn't believe I was being treated like a criminal over an honest mistake intended as a good deed. I had been Naïve. I stood in the dock, dressed smartly in my suit. I addressed the judge in a polite manner and I explained the situation to the court. I'd have had more sympathy if I was a Jew standing in front of Hitler and Himmler. I was handed a six month driving ban, points and a hefty fine. And they wonder why people hold our legal system in such contempt.

At the end of the summer, I left my position with the council and began to concentrate on the season ahead with Aberavon. I had a dream debut, my first game at the club was against Merthyr in the Welsh Cup. I came on as a second half substitute and within thirty seconds and my first touch of the ball, I scored; talk about making an impression! I followed that up by scoring in my next four appearances. Aberavon had a good squad of young up and coming local players and a few old heads with experience. I enjoyed playing there. I enjoyed playing for the coach, Chris O'Callaghan. Chris was extremely outspoken and didn't hold back if he felt you needed telling something. Chris also liked the intimidation side of the game. The ground became known as 'The World of Hurt'. A huge mural was painted on the home dressing room wall with the quote, 'In Italy, for thirty years under the Borgias, they had warfare, terror, murder and bloodshed but they produced Michelangelo, Leonardo da Vinci and the Renaissance. Meanwhile, In Switzerland, they had brotherly love, they had five hundred years of democracy and peace – and what did that produce? The fucking cuckoo clock." I loved that quote. The visiting dressing room was notorious for being less than welcoming, with hooks missing so you had nowhere to hang your clothes, freezing cold showers and the toilets were constantly blocked due to drainage issues. Things were always fine in the home dressing room though, funny that. Chris was also not scared to try out new things. One training session he told us he had ordered herbal Viagra for the players to take before games in an attempt to boost performance. I'm not sure it improved the same performance he had in mind but we tried it all the same. I liked his style of coaching and above all, he selected me most games. I was enjoying playing again; I'd had articles in the paper and complimentary things written in match reports. I finally felt I was on the right track again and that I'd made the right decision to leave Swansea. As I said, I enjoyed playing for the club as it had a good mix of up and coming players.

One of those was Sean Connolly. Sean was my brother's girlfriend's brother and other uncle to our nephew Cory. I'd known him since we were kids. I first met Sean on the Plas Newydd estate in Port Talbot. It was a rough looking place with rough people. The estate was known locally as tin town, due to the corrugated steel sheet which covered the houses. Sean had done fantastically well as he had been overweight as a youngster. He started boxing in his teens, before taking up rugby at Cwmavon Rugby Club and eventually being selected for our hometown club, Aberavon. Quite an achievement! We'd trained hard all summer as a squad, early morning sand dune training down at Merthyr Mawr, which is also used by Great British athletes due to its notorious terrain. As well as this, there was the lung busting mountain runs up the hills of Margam Park and beach running which always ended with a dip in the sea. Sean never went in the water as he couldn't swim. I liked Sean, he was bubbly, life and soul of the party and I'd usually end up dropping him off at a girl's house after training. The pre-season tour saw us travel to North Wales to play Ruthin. We travelled up on the Friday morning and arrived around early evening due to traffic. When we arrived, Chris O'Callaghan had arranged for a stop off at a local pub for something to eat. As the hotel was close by, a few of the boys, myself included, requested to stay on passed the arranged leaving time as there was a rugby league game on the TV we wanted to watch. Chris agreed on the condition that we came back after the game finished, which was scheduled for no later than 10pm. We enjoyed the game and set off with good intentions of returning early as to not upset our coach. On the short walk back, we spotted a nightclub. A suggestion to 'have a look' was made to which we all agreed we should. As is usually the case when fun is being had, we lost all track of time, and before we knew it, it was three o'clock in the morning and we were all slightly inebriated. As we were leaving, one of the boys got into an altercation with one of the locals and a fight ensued. We eventually staggered back around four o'clock, safely into bed. Chris must have had spies watching us, as the next morning there was an impromptu, early morning training session. In short,

I have never felt so sick in my life. That afternoon we beat a strong Ruthin side. Yet again, the after match shenanigans marred the tour. A few of the boys had met a few girls and been invited back to a house party. Upon arriving there, the host was far from happy when these strangers walked in and they were told to leave. An argument broke out and for the second night in a row, a mass brawl erupted. The next morning, one of the players had failed to return to the hotel and failed to make it on the bus before the instructed leaving time. Chris was quite happy to leave this player two hundred miles away in North Wales as punishment. He instructed the driver to leave. Luckily for the player in question, he arrived in a car owned by the young girl he had met the night before, just as the bus pulled out to head home. That's fantastic.

A few days later, there would be a bombshell dropped by Chris O'Callaghan, as just before the start of the season, he announced his resignation with immediate effect, and also announced a new coaching team of ex Wales internationals Kevin Hopkins and Mark Jones. I was personally devastated that Chris left when he did. I was a guaranteed starter under him. I felt as though I had been left in the lurch with his departure and wondered what the season held for me from now on in. Back on the pitch, the season had actually started well for me. I had been selected for the opening three games and Sean had been selected for two. We had a mid-week game coming up against Newport so a night out was arranged in Cardiff on the way home. Due to an injury, I wasn't selected for the game so I didn't go out as planned. Sean had tried to persuade me to come out but I declined. The next morning, I happened to drive past his dad's house and saw a police car outside. I thought nothing of it at the time. Later that morning my mam received a telephone call. I knew something wasn't right by the look on her face. I was stunned by what she told me. Sean had apparently left the other players to go and meet some friends who were studying at Cardiff University at a different bar. A short time later, a passer-by had reported seeing somebody in difficulties in the River Taff, which runs next to the Millennium Stadium. It was Sean. A search team was sent out and a body was recovered. Sadly he didn't make it. Sean died aged just 19. This had a profound effect on me. That night the players were called into the dressing room to be informed of their team mate's death. Obviously, I already knew but I had to be there anyway. It was awful. The players couldn't understand what they were being told as they had been with him not twenty four hours prior. The coaches asked if we wished to postpone the upcoming game but we decided as a squad to play on in Sean's memory. The subsequent minute silence at the next game was possibly the hardest moment of my time playing rugby. I put on a happy face and carried on as normal but inside I was hurting. I'd never lost someone close to me before and certainly not in such tragic circumstances. The funeral was attended by hundreds of people. It was a celebration of Sean's life but underneath it all there was anger that this was a needless death of someone so young. I still feel that way today.

Sean

(Above) Welsh Youth cap 2002

(Above) Taibach U'16s. 1999

Chapter Eight

'I carry the madness, everywhere I go...'

After the heartbreak of the previous months, I had booked an end of season holiday to Tenerife with Adam. We had booked a luxury hotel in the Playa de las Americas region, a five star, family resort. I couldn't wait. I was aware that the amount of alcohol we consumed would be considered excessive but this holiday reached a whole new level of absurd, especially considering the fine clientele we would soon be rubbing shoulders with. The night before our holiday, we watched in amazement as Liverpool came from three goals down at half time in the final of the Uefa Champion's League final, to level the scores shortly after the start of the second half. Liverpool went on to eventually win the match on penalties. The holiday nearly didn't happen at all, as one too many bottles of wine were consumed at the airport bar and also Adam declaring to some unfortunate passengers as we entered departures, "You better hope you're not sitting next to us, we'll terrorize you", didn't help either. Now the word, 'terror', associated with a plane and in light of the events in New York a few years previously, is not a good mix but heartfelt apologies later and we were allowed to board. We landed late at night, after a long flight, long airport transfer and with a rapidly increasing hangover. By the time we reached the hotel it was one o'clock in the morning but being sensible individuals and aware we had 7 days ahead of us, we still set out to find a bar still open late. We eventually found a backstreet bar run by two boys from Barnsley. Within the first hour we were drinking pints of vodka and red bull with a Jägermeister chaser, which was still relatively new back then. We thought it was cough medicine. We watched the sun rise from the roof terrace and headed back to the hotel. It's no exaggeration to say that whilst there we literally drank the bar's monthly supply of vodka, between two of us, in a week. One particular evening, we had gone out to watch the boxing world title fight between Ricky Hatton v Kostya Tszyu. I apparently threatened bar staff to keep serving me Bailey's, even after closing time and somehow turned up safely at the hotel on the back of a stranger's moped. I have no memory of these events but Adam reliably informs me that he literally beat me, punching me repeatedly in the face when I returned because I would not stop talking incoherent nonsense. Once the beating was dished out, I was placed in the hotel bath, where Adam caringly covered me in flowers and newspapers and then posed for photographs whilst I was blissfully unaware in my alcohol induced coma. What are friends for? The carnage continued. One night, Adam somehow managed to injure his foot whilst attempting to kick innocent cockroaches as they scurried across the promenade floor. Families looked on in disgust as Adam hollered "Alan Shearer" at each wild swing at his intended target. As fate would have it and Karma for the cockroaches, Adam missed, instead, he kicked the marble floor. His toe was badly cut. By now, we had an audience of disapproving holiday makers watching from the hotel balconies. The next morning, Adam's toe was severely swollen. He decided to try and heal his injured foot in the swimming pool with a method that would be known as 'the salt wound routine.' Upon placing his injured, badly cut toe, into the salt water pool, he screamed, "Ahhh, my salt wound routine!" at the top of his lungs. Fellow guests looked in shock and concern as Adam hobbled out of the pool, limping, like an injured wildebeest, before safely resting on the comfort of his sun lounger. This outburst would be the final straw with hotel management following other numerous complaints. The behaviour was so bad that by the third night we had a security escort, whom were waiting for us upon our arrival from our night out, to take us safely up to our rooms in an orderly fashion. As we were fine considerate, upstanding gentlemen of the community, we decided to pull up some flowers from outside the hotels' beautifully arranged floral beds and offer them to our chaperones as thanks, upon reaching the lobby. Just as we thought, we approached the hotel and Pedro and his merry men were waiting for us. Adam offered up the freshly picked bouquet and lovingly stated, "Flowers for you, my darling." Pedro did not see the funny side and threatened to draw his baton. Luckily for us, he thought better of it and instead, aggressively marched us back to our room before placing his fingers on his lips to encourage us to be quiet. This routine continued for the remaining few nights we were there. I'm surprised I wasn't almost deported from Spain for a second time.

The holiday ended with us saying goodbye to the Barnsley boys, thanking them for their hospitality. We checked out of our hotel at midday but as our flight wasn't until 2:00am we decided against drinking that day. This agreement lasted a full ten minutes until we got to the bar. More vodka red bulls and sampling the local beer was in order before being treated to a vindaloo by our kind Yorkshire hosts to say our final farewells. After twelve hours of drinking vodka and a belly full of spicy curry, what followed was the most horrendous flight since 9/11. During the four hour journey, Adam did not utter a single word to me, or when we arrived back in Cardiff or even on the bus journey back to Port Talbot. What sounds like hell to me now, was one of the best holidays ever.

Upon returning home, Adam and I continued to enjoy our nights out. One Sunday afternoon, I met up with two brothers from our Taibach days, Leon and Dean, as well as Craig Clements and Reggie. We met in The Twelve Knights pub in Margam. The afternoon started out fairly respectable, a few quiet drinks whilst watching the football. As the days went on, pints had been replaced for bottles of wine. Somebody then produced a bottle of poppers, otherwise known as rush. The sale and consumption of this are perfectly legal as 'poppers' are usually sold as a room odorizer but are commonly used for a different purpose. The following sentence, taken from an online source gives an idea of the intended usage and why it's commonly abused.

'First produced in 1857 as a treatment for angina, amyl nitrite evaporates at room temperature. The vapour released causes your veins and arteries to dilate resulting in the blood flowing faster through the heart and the brain. On the dancefloor it feels like you've been hit by a percussive thunderbolt and if you're having sex it feels like your sexual organs have grown to Herculean proportions. The effect only lasts for a few moments and you might feel a little light headed for a minute or so afterwards'

A game was devised where you had to drink your beverage, inhale the rush for ten seconds, and then be prepared to be interrogated. The results were hilarious. The mix of alcohol coupled with the head rush and quick fire questions made you forget your own name. People were falling off chairs and struggling to breathe because of the laughter. We were no doubt damaging ourselves in search of fun but at the time, it wasn't a concern. It was around this time that another male joined our group. I'd known Michael Mulhern or Buller as he's more commonly known, from school. He slotted in perfectly because he was an instigator of many wonderful adventures. Michael certainly wasn't the biggest of the group but I'd make him the most aggressive and certainly most volatile. By then, we had earned a certain level of respect in the pubs around town; not in a bad way, but everyone knew who we were, partly down to being well known through rugby, and partly down to the fact that it didn't take much to provoke individuals, especially Buller. That said, he had a fantastic sense of humour and as I said, we had some great adventures together. It was after leaving the local nightclub with Buller, that we realized we had no money for a taxi. We didn't live all that far but it was cold and had started to rain. As we walked to take shelter, we came across a girl who was feeling unwell in a doorway. Not wanting to leave the girl, we called for medical assistance and an ambulance arrived. I had mentioned to Buller that the ambulance would make a great taxi, as the hospital in Port Talbot was only around the corner from where we lived. We could hop out once there and continue on home. The girl's condition worsened, by now she appeared to be unconscious so the paramedic asked if we friends of the unfortunate stranger. I don't know why but we looked at each other, shrugged our shoulder and replied, "Yes." We hopped in the ambulance and began our short journey. It was after maybe fifteen minutes that we mentioned the drive was taking an unusually long time. The paramedic informed us that we were on our way to

Bridgend Hospital, which is about twenty miles from our intended destination. Great, we were in a worse position that when we started. We arrived at the hospital and were taken straight to a cubicle. By now the poor girl had regained consciousness and thankfully was fine, which was a good thing because we had no idea who she was, so we could not inform the nurses of her name. Feeling that our good deed was partly done, we made our escape. We headed back to the main doors and tried to think of a way to get home to Port Talbot. Whilst we were thinking, we took the opportunity to have a quick wheelchair race up and down the long hospital corridors. We even went for a late night snack in the canteen, before hospital security caught up with us and asked to leave. After the fun, we decided the only way back home was to get a taxi. As I mentioned earlier, the only problem with that was, we didn't actually have any money for the long journey. We eventually found a driver willing to take us the twenty miles home and promised him payment on arrival. We approached Margam, a part of town near the local steelworks and about a mile from the town centre so we asked the driver to stop there as we had reached our destination. In the blink of an eye we were out of the doors, over the wall and running along the backstreets. We knew we wouldn't get caught from there. We congratulated ourselves on a job well done, then realized five hours had passed since we first left the club. We were now soaking wet and still further away from where we had originally began.

I would later have another incident with a taxi. I and a boy named Matthew Rowlands had taken a taxi home after a night out. We arrived outside my parents' house and the driver asked for payment. We looked at each other as I assumed he was paying, he told me that he assumed I was paying and without warning, Matthew opened the doors and ran away. Before I could even react, the driver locked the doors. The driver angrily suggested that I knock on my parent's door and ask them for the £6 I owed for the short journey. Being slightly worse for wear, I declined his reasonable offer, as I didn't want to wake my sleeping parents. The driver informed me that if I didn't come up with the payment, that he would simply take me to the police station. I thought momentarily about the repercussions and replied, "Well so be it." My fate was sealed. Not for the first time and not for the last time and off the back of my own stupidity, I would spend the night in a police cell. To make matters worse, the following morning after my release, I still had to pay another taxi driver to take me home from the police station, in Neath, nearly ten miles away from my home. All in all, it cost me triple the original amount I owed to the first taxi driver. Looking back, I don't condone my behaviour back then, and if I knew the drivers from those nights, I would happily reimburse them. That said, desperate times required desperate measures.

(Below) Me and Adam. Tenerife. 2005

(Above) Me, Adam and David Flynn

(Below) Great hairstyles!

Chapter Nine

'Moving away, and though there's a new lifeline, I won't forget the one that I left behind...'

After a disappointing previous season with Aberavon, in which I'd spent the majority on dual contract with Corus RFC, I decided to leave. The last few months of the season would be a calamity. One afternoon, whilst playing for Corus, I unwittingly told a Welsh rugby legend to 'Fuck Off.' We were playing in the Carmarthenshire village of Felinfoel. It was a horrible, wet, windy day. Our winger had to go off injured early in the game, so I was asked to cover the position. Usually I wouldn't have minded but considering the conditions, I knew I wouldn't be seeing much of the ball and didn't look forward to standing out in the pissing down rain, freezing my bollocks off. Predictably, this is exactly what happened. Throughout the first half, a small, older man on the side line kept telling me to 'push up' 'cover back' and encouraged me to 'go looking for the ball.' I soon began to grow tired of his constant orders. I turned around and said, "Why don't you just fuck off! What do you know anyway?" It turned out that little old man who knew nothing was Welsh rugby legend and possibly the finest outside half of all time, Phil Bennett. Actually, I did listen to Phil's advice in the second half; I did go looking for the ball and ended up scoring the only try of a low scoring game. It turned out to be the winner, cheers Phil.

The unfortunate mishaps continued. I'd injured my leg during a 'sevens' tournament down the Aberavon Green Stars. The pitch was ridiculously dry and I ended up with grass burns. Instead of seeking medical advice, I left the wound to puss and fester for over a week. Not only did I stick to the sheets of a night but by now, the smell was overwhelming. I went to the doctors and was told it was now badly infected. The hospital scrapped the dead skin off and I was placed in an iodine bath, not the most pleasant experience. To make matters even worse, I also broke the tip of my finger in the same tournament, Christ, it was supposed to be fun these sevens tournaments - not for me. My final league game for Aberavon was against a team called Pontypridd, notorious for being a difficult place to play. I started on the bench. I'd become increasingly unhappy with my bit part for the team. I felt I had so much to offer but my face didn't seem to fit with the new coaches. Towards the end of the game I was told to warm up as I was going on. It's hard to motivate yourself from the bench and as the game was already lost, I have to be honest, my head wasn't right. I took to the field at a lineout, five meters out from our own try line. The ball was overthrown and landed behind me, as I'd just walked on the pitch, I wasn't yet match sharp so reacted slowly. My opposite number reacted quicker and approached the bouncing ball at speed. He was sure to score so I not only pulled back his jersey but tripped him up as well. The ref had no hesitation in giving me a yellow card; I'd only been on the pitch twenty seconds. I walked off for my ten minutes in the sin bin, despondent. The team bench was on the far side of the pitch so I stood contemplating my choices on the near touch line. I should have chosen a better spot for my daydreaming as I was now directly in front the famously vocal support of the Sardis Road crowd. I received a bit of light hearted abuse, "Oh, Butt! You're fucking shit mun." I should have ignored it but I didn't. I responded by giving the crowd the middle finger. The ironic, piss taking cheer went up. They had got the reaction they wanted from me. Not content with this, I then felt a warm sensation on the back of my head. I glanced down and realized that someone had thrown a meat pie at me, I couldn't believe it; those pies cost a fortune at matches. It was a frustrating way to end my time with Aberavon but this trend was becoming alarmingly familiar.

I had a few offers from teams in the Premiership but it was Carmarthen Quins I decided to start the following season with and mainly because they offered the most money. Carmarthen was a two hour round trip from Port Talbot. At first I didn't mind the journey because as luck would have it, a good friend of mine, James Jones had also signed for Carmarthen Quins. As I've mentioned before, I played for both Taibach and Aberavon with James, he was always good company so I welcomed his arrival. Our first journey down to training was a disaster. Neither of us knew the area we were heading and I didn't have a Satnav. We ended up being late by quite some time. Pre-season went quite well, however, I didn't like the pod system of hitting rucks the coach was insisting on. I prefer to play my own game. I had the fitness to get around the field and I didn't like being dictated to as what I could and couldn't do. To me, this was taking away players' natural instincts. Even still, I went ahead with his wishes. I'd started the opening two league games, scoring in both, when I picked up a slight injury. It was nothing serious, but during my two weeks off, I had received another offer which excited me. I dropped my own bombshell by declaring my intentions to move to Manchester. I felt that after the incidents in the previous year, that I had to live my life, explore different things. Plus I felt my life was spiralling out of control, I felt I was neglecting my rugby ability; I was in and out of the team, I had run in's with coaches. It seemed my whole focus in life was to make it to the next weekend with the boys. I needed to regain my focus. I'd been put in touch with Wayne Morris; he was originally from Port Talbot, but now living in Sale, Manchester. Wayne had previously played rugby for Aberavon but was now coaching a team called Altrincham Kersals. It was agreed that I would come up, play for them, whilst also training with the Sale Sharks academy. Accommodation was provided and I was to live with a boy from Barnsley. Now, the less said about my time in Manchester the better. To say that it didn't live up to an expectation is an understatement. I didn't know the area, my housemate was constantly away so I was constantly alone, I sat for hours watching box sets and to top it off, the standard of rugby at Altrincham was poor. I'd played in the three pre-season games and it was too easy for me. There was no challenge whatsoever; I'd be running past people like they weren't even there. I thrive on a battle and it was obvious that there was no battle to be had here. It was extremely different to the professional standard pitches and facilities I was used to back in Wales. I was frustrated but decided to stay to see if things improve. They didn't.

Adam came up to stay with me, as did my brothers. We had some good nights out but if anything this made the situation worse. I was homesick. I started going out on my own, into the city centre. I'd sit in pubs and people watch, I was turning into a bloody loner. One night I got chatting to a man whilst putting songs on the jukebox. He seemed clued up on the songs I was selecting so we started discussing bands. We had a few drinks together and he invited me back to his house to meet his friends, have a few beers and to listen to some music. He seemed a bit odd but keen to see more of Manchester and having just enough alcohol in my system, I agreed. A bus journey later and we arrived in Moss Side, Manchester. The area looked like it was twinned with Beirut, with boarded up windows, a burnt out car, a pair of trainers dangling from the telephone line above and police on every street corner. We called into the shop to get some cans of lager and made our way to his house. I started to sober up and began to feel uneasy. Something didn't feel right. When we got to the house, it had a metal shutter where the front door should have been and similarly boarded windows. He made his way inside with me following. I couldn't believe my eyes, it wasn't a home; it was a shell of a house. Downstairs was only bare brick and exposed floorboards. I couldn't even make out any noticeable rooms. It was a mess. There were no lights so he lit candles, and as there were no chairs, we sat on the floor. I noticed a lot of cans thrown around and a sleeping bag on the floor. It soon became apparent he was squatting there. By now I definitely felt the urge to get out. The bloke's whole demeanour changed and he started asking lots of questions about where I was living. I told him I was staying in Altrincham, which is in a rich area of Manchester and that I was here to play rugby. He seemed intrigued by this and wanted to know how much money I had. I dismissed the question by laughing and saying I was effectively a student and therefore, penniless. The atmosphere by now was moody to say the very least. I asked where the bathroom was, I didn't need to go but I thought I could make my escape whilst there. I was told, quite assertively, there was no bathroom. He began rambling about how life had been unfair to him. I replied saying life can be cruel, he nodded in agreement and again, he asked how much money I had on me. By now I was actually scared so informed him more aggressively that I already told him I had nothing on me. I could see he was getting agitated but he tried to make a joke out of the situation by saying he was only messing and to calm down. My instincts heightened, I could feel the blood pumping through my body. I again asked where I could use the bathroom. This time he got up and attempted to block the doorway. He was laughing but he said, "You're not going anywhere." I didn't need to think twice, I ran at the bloke. I was aware I was considerably bigger than him; I managed to throw him to one side and run down the stairs. As luck would have it, the shutter door was still already open so I ran out and into the street. I didn't even look back. I didn't know where I was and adrenalin was running through my whole body. Luckily I found a bus stop just as a bus arrived. I didn't even know where it was going but I got on. Still feeling a sense of panic, I returned to my house. I have no idea what his intentions were or if he had done that before but his mannerisms were not those of somebody that had good wishes towards me. I felt shook up by the whole experience and have never really talked about it since, partly because of my own stupidity to go with a complete stranger into a house I already had doubts about. Thankfully I was able to over-power him, otherwise, who knows what may have happened. A short time later, I decided Manchester was not for me. I returned home, completely disillusioned and with my tail firmly between my legs. Such was my disappointment with life in Manchester that I can't even recount another single thing of note to mention. Perhaps, it rained, a lot, will suffice. I'd been home for a few months when I got a call from my old coach at Aberavon, Chris O'Callaghan. Prior to this, I'd agreed to join my old junior team, the Aberavon Green Stars. A local builder, Nigel Trott, was now bank rolling the Division Three side and offered me a sizeable match fee, as well as a full time position with his local construction firm. I couldn't turn the offer down. He had signed some good players and promotion was inevitable given the standard of the squad. I'd played in maybe a dozen games and again, the standard of rugby was too easy for me. I'd score tries for fun. Without being disrespectful to players at that level, it was nothing more than an ego boost for me. It didn't take long before I had slipped back into my old habits of drinking too much on the weekend with friends. Myself, Adam, Hibbard, David Dyers, Dan Williams and Michael Mulhern caused that much disruption in the local Weatherspoon's that we actually had door staff standing near our table when we arrived, just in case things got out of hand. Inevitably they would. Lights were pulled off the wall, ice cubes thrown around and even a fire extinguisher was set off by Michael Mulhern on the stairs. He also followed this up a few years later by setting off a fire extinguisher in a taxi on the way to a Christmas night out in Swansea, covering everyone inside in foam. It was becoming his signature move. Things appeared to be going nowhere again. One evening, I received a call from Chris O'Callaghan, enquiring as to why I was now wasting my talents in the lower levels of rugby. He said he was scouting for the newly formed rugby league club, the Celtic Crusaders and offered me a trial week. I had played briefly in the past for Aberavon Fighting Irish. I attended training and for the most parts, I enjoyed it. Rugby league is quicker than rugby union and that suited me. The only problem I had was what position I would actually play. My position in Union means covering lots of ground, being the first to the breakdown; basically, being a link man between backs and forwards. There was no such position in League as they play with two less players than the union game. During the training games, I'd constantly follow the ball across the pitch instead of getting back into my channel. I also struggled to adapt to having to retreat ten yards after every tackle. It seems simple but when you've done the opposite for fifteen years it doesn't come naturally. After the end of the week I decided that rugby league wasn't for me.

About two months later, I got another call from Chris. He wanted to arrange a meeting to discuss moving to a club he'd taken over. I met him at the Twelve Knights Hotel, Margam. Chris being Chris sold the idea to me straight away. His plans were to take this team to the Premiership of English rugby. He had big signings lined up, a potential ground move, top training facilities, and he apparently had the backing to do it. The only problem was he hadn't told me who this team was! All he asked me was, "Would you be up for moving to Waterloo?'" and my honest response was, "Yes, I wouldn't mind living in London." I later learnt that Waterloo was in fact in Liverpool, not London. It didn't take me too long to make a decision. By the end of the week, I was off again. On the train journey up, Chris had texted me to say 'when you get here, you'll meet the Mayor, he'll be waiting. There might be a band playing as well.' As it was, upon getting off the train, I was greeted by a fat man with a card which simply said 'Bradley'. I assumed he wasn't the Mayor and my suspicions were confirmed, as he didn't have a band with him. My initial disappointments were again compounded, when I was told my new accommodation was 'a wooden cabin behind the posts' my initial joy at seeing, what can only be described as a mansion, soon turned to horror as my driver said "there you go" nodding in the opposite direction to where I had been looking, instead, pointing towards a shack that looked like it had severe woodworm, loose slates on the roof and green algae covering the cladding. My optimism was not helped upon meeting my so called housemates either; posh Dan, from Cheltenham, who thought anybody who didn't attend public school was a peasant and Argentinian, Bruno. A 20 stone prop who put his shit (yes, excrement) into the waste bin instead of flushing it. The flat was a wonderful array of accents though. My particular favourite would be Bruno telling Dan to 'shut up, fucking prick' in a flamboyant way that only a Latin American could, when questioned as to why his dirty socks and jock strap were placed on the dining table. I think deep down they loved each other really. It didn't show. I took Bruno under my wing. At the tender age of 22, I was seen as the father figure in the flat. Bruno spoke very little English so I was designated as the person to teach him the language, as well as inform him of the ways of British life. I found it ironic that they had chosen a boy from the deepest depths of South Wales to teach somebody English; I could barely speak the language properly myself. My teachings obviously didn't work as one evening, he was driving the club vehicle, with me in the passenger seat, when he approached a roundabout. Instead of staying in the left lane to go around, he drifted onto the right side of the roundabout, into oncoming traffic and exited on the wrong side of the road. It later turned out, twelve months later, that Bruno never actually had a valid license. He had used his brother's Argentinian license as a form of identification. The pre-season was good, hard, intense, but fun as well. At the time we had ex Rugby League legend Joe Lydon as performance consultant. I liked Joe; he knew the game and knew how to make me a better player. We had team video sessions and even a booklet was handed out with information on our opponents the following game, informing us of danger men, line out calls and backline moves. I had to adapt to the English game. In Wales, the game is freely flowing, running rugby. In England, it was tight, forward based and physical. I felt good, fit, and headed over to Ireland for our first pre-season game against Garryowen from the Munster region. At Liverpool airport, one of the players forgot his passport, a South African named David Yorke. As there was no time to head back to collect his travel document, we assumed he'd miss the flight. Dave didn't seem too concerned with this news and made a quick call. He came back confidently saying it would be sorted. Within ten minutes he had an emergency travel document for the flight. It turned out his dad worked as a diplomat for the South African government. We stayed in the Munster Universities' Halls of Residence. The set up was fantastic. The sports department there was designed for professionals and it showed. Fitness testing, pool recovery, healthy meals and body fat checks. It's amazing to see how far rugby has advanced in such a short space of time. While we were in Ireland, we heard the sad news from Liverpool, about little Rhys Jones who was shot and killed after being caught in the crossfire of rival gangs. The game itself went well. I was surprised to see ex-Welsh international Chris Wyatt playing for the Irish side. I thought he had retired years ago. His experience still made him a class player and he was definitely a handful on that day. The opposition also had current Ireland international scrum half, Connor Murray playing that day. It was supposed to be a friendly but it was anything but. I remember a huge brawl in which everybody got involved, all thirty players and subs too. It got quite ugly and spilt over into the stand. I could see Chris O'Callaghan was itching to get involved. You might think a team brawl is not important but it shows the team spirit was there from an early stage. The good thing about Waterloo was all the players were of a similar age, early twenties and a similar situation, having moved to the area from as far afield as Australia, South Africa and Argentina. A few weeks into the season and the club signed the current Spanish sevens captain, Pablo Feijoo, as well as

Nicola Mazzucato, who had recently been involved in the 2007 Rugby World Cup for Italy and ex Llanelli scarlets player Aled Gravelle. I liked Aled as he was a no-nonsense player who added a bit of steel to the pack. He was also great to have around the club. He added to the growing Welsh contingent already at Waterloo and for me that was not a bad thing. I have never attended university but I imagine that is what it would be like; people from different walks of life, different cultures and new experiences. It was a turning point in my life.

I'd been in Liverpool a few weeks when I invited Adam up for the weekend. As it was the summer holidays and Adam was now a teacher, he agreed. One afternoon we were having a few drinks with my other flat mates when someone suggested a game of football. The game started off sensibly enough, but soon descended into chaos. As it was a hot summer's day, we started off by playing topless but by the end of the game, most were bollock naked. I have no idea why this was the case, but it was, and I have no explanation to give you on the matter. Later that evening, a committee member approached me and told me that the old lady next door had phoned to complain. Apparently she looked out the window upon hearing a commotion next door and was greeted by six pricks, literally. I had to pop round with flowers and tell this fragile old dear that we were new to the house and were getting to know each other and that we were deeply sorry for any offence caused and hope we didn't upset her. Luckily she saw the funny side, I'm even sure she winked at me.

I was soon joined at Waterloo by James Jones. As I have mentioned, I had played most of my career with James and I was glad when he arrived, and as I've also mentioned, James is a fantastic character and slotted right in at Waterloo. I give him this glowing character reference, despite the fact that whilst playing against him for my school, he broke my wrist with a bad tackle. I forgave him though. Things soon settled down very quickly. I felt at home. I was helped immensely by local builder and Waterloo supporter, Dave Morris. Dave offered me a job as a labourer and I will always appreciate how welcome Dave, Deb, Dan, Ellie and Henry made me feel, even if I did neglect his good will gesture by phoning in sick every Monday morning. It had absolutely nothing whatsoever to do with Sunday nights out in the village. Honestly. As is compulsory for most teams, new players had to undergo an initiation process to welcome them to their new club. I'm sure most have seen videos of the footballers version of singing a song or performing a dance and that is deemed acceptable? Well, a rugby initiation is very different. Our initiation occurred on the team bus after an away game. The ritual involved the captain, a mountain of a man known as, Cakes, introducing the new players one by one. We had to strip, completely naked and walk up and down the aisle of the bus while the other players took it in turns to slap your arse as hard as they could. Far from being over, we then had to take our place on the back seat of the bus, still naked. We were offered the choice of a cider drink or lager drink and told to take the persons next to you boxer shorts and place the arse end over the can. As luck would have it, I was placed next to my, twenty stone, Argentinian flatmate, Bruno. He gleefully handed me his match worn under-garments, still damp from the sweat and I placed them over the can. We were told that this was a race between us and the losers would face a punishment. I soon encountered a problem; the flow of alcohol was to slow and in order to obtain any liquid from the can I would have to suck enthusiastically through the boxer shorts. I think I'd have preferred the impending forfeit. Predictably, I lost and my punishment was to drink four shots in a row. This didn't seem so bad at the time, I was handed a carrier bag and told to be sick in there. I couldn't work out why I would need the bag or why I would need to be sick but then it became apparent. The captain produced four bottles; Aftershock, Absinthe,

Grappa and Poitin, the last two are both 90% proof alcohol and told to drink, one by one. It is safe to say that I made good use of the plastic bag provided and I will forever be haunted by the taste experienced at the back of the bus, including Bruno's arse.

The first season went well. I enjoyed travelling down to Cornwall, London, Durham, and staying in nice hotels. These were new places to me. I had complete independence for the first time properly and I was making the most of it. We finished 5th with an incredibly young team, the average being 22 with the oldest player being 28. We'd beaten the teams above us home and away but lost some tough fixtures in winter. The muddy pitches against teams with a big pack of forwards would be our undoing. We did enjoy some success that season as we won the Lancashire Cup, beating a team from the league above, on their own ground, in the final. I scored the winning try that day. I finished the season with eleven tries in all competitions and again, had some nice comments from supporters, newspaper articles and felt the fittest and strongest I have ever been. I was still enjoying nights out after the game but I felt I had the right balance. Maybe that's what had been missing for all the years previous? I knew it wasn't my ability that was the problem; it always seemed to be my attitude that was being questioned.

Looking back, I know I had a fear of making mistakes, I still do. I'm also quite an outspoken person and would usually answer back to any constructive criticism aimed my way. Still, I felt optimistic for the future. I was 22, still young and still had genuine hopes of playing regional rugby in Wales. I planned to use my time in England to adapt my game. I knew my attacking ability was fine, which was basically my game; speed, support, scoring tries, these skills came naturally to me. I wanted to build on my defensive skills. I knew that English rugby would be a lot more physical so I looked forward to the challenge. Personally I felt a massive improvement was made in my first season. I was fortunate to play in a strong back row and we complimented each other well. The forthcoming season would be a massive one for me, a season to kick on and really become the player I wanted to be. As fate would have it, that would be my last full season at a top level. A serious shoulder injury in a pre-season game, down In Port Talbot of all places, would be a reoccurring problem which would result in full shoulder reconstruction. We'd travelled down to Wales to face Tonmawr and Aberavon, two teams I had previously played for. Again, pre-season had gone well. I'd enjoyed it. We'd had a former member of the military, Mark Godwin to train us and it worked. Mark brought in sandbags and bodyweight exercises. There was no long distance running, it was short, sharp and intense to replicate the match scenarios. We worked a lot on attack and defence and the team looked sharp going into the new season. We were fitter, faster than the season before. I couldn't wait to play Tonmawr, I felt I had a point to prove. I didn't, but the circumstances I left in made me want to prove something to myself - that I'd made the right choice. My family and friends including Hibbard came to watch and when the game started I felt like a man possessed, making tackles, running with the ball, I felt in my best shape ever. Then mid-way through the first half, the outside half attempted a kick and I went to charge it down. I instinctively put my arm out to block it, I did, the ball landed over the try line and I fell on it to score. Due to the adrenaline I briefly felt nothing, then I felt a rush of pain and realized my arm had popped out of the socket. The physio immediately popped it back in and made me come off. I didn't want to leave the field. I watched on, happy that the boys had won the game but disappointed for myself. That night I was in agony. I didn't sleep at all. I missed the next game against Aberavon. I was devastated. Despite the injury, I managed to play the first game of the league season a few days later. This was mainly at the request of Chris. I knew I was in no condition to play, but I dosed myself up with painkillers. The opening game was a disaster; we were well beaten by the Cornish Pirates. A good, well organized team, who would gain promotion that season. I asked to come off at half time, I was in agony. Chris blamed me for the opening try as I had missed a tackle on their centre. He accused me of bottling it because we were losing. I was furious. He'd known me for a long time and one thing I am not is a coward. A few harsh words were exchange, and I refused to go out for the second half. I sat in the changing room feeling numb; I knew this injury would rule me out for a while. This would be the last time I would speak to Chris O'Callaghan. He left the club by mutual consent the next day. To this day, I have had no contact with him. It does make me sad that a coach, a man I held in high regard, can hold a grudge from one incident, after years of service to him. I hope one day we can have a few drinks together and look back on that as a bad day for both of us. A few days later, I reluctantly went for the MRI scan, I say reluctantly because I knew something wasn't right but I wasn't expecting the diagnosis either. I'd torn my bicep, tricep, front and rear deltoid and pectoral muscle off the bone. The specialist told me I'd miss the whole season as surgery was required. It floored me, the season had only just started, yet it had finished for me after only forty minutes. A whole summer's training for this important season, gone. The surgery went well; painful but a success nonetheless. I started physio weeks ahead of schedule. In my mind I'd be back before the end of the season. I'd had injuries and rushed back before the recommended time. I'd previously severed a tendon in my hand and was put in a cast with an iron bar holding my hand in place. Three months I was told I'd miss. Two weeks later I strapped it up heavily and played in an important end of season game. I had to get it stitched up again as they had come out and opened the wound up again. I had a track record for this, cutting the casts off broken wrists to play, before going back the next day to have it put back on. This is why I never understood coaches questioning my commitment; I'd do anything to play. I'd even risk further damage to myself to get out on the pitch. To me, that's not a lack of commitment that, at worst, is stupidity.

As I mentioned, my biggest issue was failure. Or fear of failure I should say. I'd set high standards for myself and would crucify myself if I had a poor game. Maybe not publicly, but inside, I'd run it over and over in my head. Even the slightest thing would eat away at me until I was terrified to try it again in case I fucked up again. If a particular move that I'd cocked up was brought up in training, I'd have a little stretch on the side line, just to avoid doing it. Eventually I avoided any type of set team move in training, in case I run the wrong line or forget which way left and right was. It sounds ludicrous but that's how bad it became. If I simply avoided doing it, I didn't have to worry about my confidence between shot to bits - it was a coping mechanism. As I mentioned, I'd played on through injuries in the past and I thought this would be the same but I didn't realize how severe this injury was. I literally had to learn to use my arm again, it was dead for months. I had to sleep sitting bolt upright because if I lay down, I couldn't get back up. It was agonisingly slow. Eight months later, I had full movement again, my weights were increasing and I started running. Gradually, it involved full contact again in training. I had got myself back to full fitness inside twelve months; I was ready to go again. Things would prove frustrating as during my injury, Waterloo Rugby Club had come into money troubles. It was well-known and the Committee made no effort to disguise the problems, however, nobody was expecting the club to announce, just a few weeks before the start of the season that it had gone bankrupt. Various members of the club tried to blame Chris O'Callaghan as it was him that had brought players to the club offering them good money, before eventually quitting. But to me, the issue was the board not supporting Chris's earlier visions and failing to think big for the future of the club. The idea was put forward that Waterloo should sell the land the ground was built on, as potential developers would pay a huge amount to secure it. Properties in the area were amongst the highest in the North West. The clubs current ground was indeed, charming, with its huge, open fire in the main bar, or the famous player's lounge in which on match day, you were loudly cheered through as you walked out on to the pitch. The area where the ground is was not right to develop a fan base. Most of the people of Liverpool didn't even know who Waterloo were, let alone know where the ground was. Chris wanted to take the club out to the suburbs, away from the quiet, leafy, well-to-do area it resides in. With the potential money raised, the club could buy land owned by Everton Football Club. The site was their former training ground, right in the middle of a working class housing estate with good links to motorways and surrounding areas. Waterloo could have built a new, modern stadium, suitable for the clubs aspirations of top flight rugby. The choices were simple - move and give the club the chance to prosper; the potential to be the sole club in Merseyside or stay where they were and risk becoming a team destined to stay in the lower leagues, existing solely to please the regulars in the cosy clubhouse. Just before Chris resigned, an AGM was called to decide the clubs fate. The members overwhelmingly rejected the proposals in favour of staying where they were. This would eventually mean that the standard the club wanted to reach was not sustainable against the money they were paying for players, hence the sudden bankruptcy. Some teams in the league were getting attendances in their thousands, Waterloo were in the low hundreds. It was a traditional club, well respected due to producing some well-known players who'd represented England, namely, Will Greenwood, Ben Kay and Austin Healey. These players came through at a time when rugby was still an amateur sport but rugby was now professional, with high match fees and travel and accommodation costs. Inevitably the money was going to run out. When told about the bankruptcy, the players I had played with mostly returned to their counties of origin. At first I was annoyed that they wouldn't stay and fight for the club. But at the same time, they had no commitment to the club. If they weren't getting paid what they were offered, why would they stay? In the following weeks at training, the squad was unrecognizable. The club was expecting young boys with no experience and in truth, very little quality at that level, to travel around the country, play against top class teams and to do a job. I remember having a conversation with a particular committee man and he told me that he thought it may be a blessing in disguise as there were some good young players coming through the ranks, who had been pushed down to second or third team level unfairly over somebody who's not even from this area, who are only here because of the money and doesn't play for the pride of the jersey. Despite this being an obvious pop at me, I overlooked his comment and instead I told him that I completely disagreed and without being disrespectful that the local players were nowhere near good enough and never will be. After playing with top quality players for most of my career, you soon learn who's got what it takes to play at that level, and who hasn't and I'm sad to say, these boys didn't. I took no satisfaction in my comments being right as we were losing games heavily, in some instances, by over a hundred points. It was demoralizing. With a heavy heart, I made the decision to leave Waterloo, fearing this was a sinking ship, which later proved to be the case. Waterloo was relegated four years in a row and now plays in the amateur leagues of Northern England. The club will always be close to me, even though I was there for a relatively short period of playing time. They were very accommodating to me in my first season and I will always be grateful for that support. The club now appears to be at a level comfortable to them, producing mainly local players through its junior section. I wish them all the best for the future.

I was soon approached by another National League side, Caldy which is situated in an affluent area on the Wirral. Again, my time here would prove extremely short. In only my second game, and right at the end of the match, I received the ball from kick off. I turned my back as the ball dropped over my shoulder and felt an impact. There was no malicious intent whatsoever; it was just one of those things that can easily happen in a contact sport. In the changing room, I started to get agonising back spasms. I decided a nice warm shower would ease this. Once in the shower and, as is customary, I began to urinate on the floor below, however I soon noticed that my urine was an odd colour, not the dark yellow shade when you are severely dehydrated, but red. I was pissing blood. This sight, I can tell you, is quite alarming so, again, I took myself to hospital. After so many recent visits I was on first name terms with most of the staff. I was even sure they would offer me my own parking space. I met the consultant and the prognosis was a ruptured kidney. So again, I was side-lined. The problem I began to face was that all the friends I had originally made had more or less; all left the club and moved away from the area. Before this I was constantly surrounded by players of a similar ability, who loved the game. Suddenly I looked around and there was nobody I could relate to. All my other friends were football fans; they didn't like rugby, as was the case for the most of Merseyside as rugby is a minor sport. With no involvement or interaction, I found it increasingly difficult to motivate myself. Whilst I was recovering, I stopped going to watch the games, nobody called or text to see where I was and I slipped completely under the radar. I put on weight and as a result wanted to distance myself even further from people who knew me. At the time I was injured, I was approached by Clive Griffiths, an ex-Wales international coach, who was coaching the newly formed RGC 1404 in North Wales. He was after a pacey open side flanker that suited the attacking team they were building over in Colwyn Bay. I liked the vision he had for the club. He had brought good coaches in and was playing at the Eirias Stadium which had fantastic facilities. Arrangements had been made to travel across to North Wales once my injury had healed and I initially agreed to the move. I had told him that I hadn't played in a long time, over a year by this point and that I had put on a lot of weight. Even still, he was keen to get me involved. Potentially it could have been another stepping stone, I was still only 24, I had years to get myself back on track but I soon started doubting myself. I had convinced myself that I was no longer good enough, that my pace had gone and that I'd be found out at that level now. I was again, too hard on myself. I'd listened to the voices in my head so I took the easy way out. I decided that, at the age of 24 that I would retire from a game I ultimately loved. I hadn't made it official but in my head, it was over.

(Below) Waterloo RFC. 2007/2008

(Below) Me Bruno celebrate winning the Lancashire cup with Waterloo in 2008.

(Above) Waterloo changing rooms after beating Garryowen in Ireland 2007

(Below) Celebrating a try.

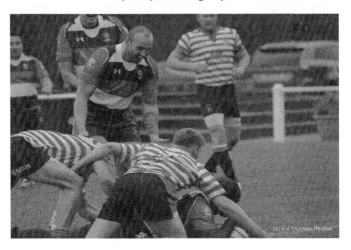

Chapter Ten

'Where were you while we were getting high...?'

This is the chapter where my life would start to take, what you could call, some normality, only some though. In 2010, and a few months after deciding rugby was no longer for me, I was working with a landscape gardener. I knew the owner of the company from my time with Dave Morris Builders. I had contacted him to see if there was any work available and to be fair, he gave me a job, but he gave me a role that could only be described as a dogsbody. The hours were shit and the pay even worse. In the meantime, I had applied for hundreds of jobs, not really sure of what sector really suited me and it appeared I wasn't in the position to be too picky, after nothing but rejections. I was amazed to receive a telephone call, inviting me for an interview for a position at the HMRC tax office in Bootle. On the day of the interview, I dressed to impress, buying a new suit and shoes specifically for the day. I arrived early and was told to wait in reception. I looked around and all I could think was that those also waiting to be seen looked far more intelligent than me, whatever look that is. My name was called and I was greeted by a stern looking male. I was escorted into the interview room. He opened my curriculum vitae, studied it for a moment, before questioning me on my rugby background. "Do you like Wigan Warriors?" a rugby league team who play in the Super League. It seemed like a bizarre opening question but I proceeded to confirm that I did, picking up that the man had a strong Lancashire accent and not wishing to disappoint or offend him. It seemed to go down well with my interviewer and for ten minutes we talked about nothing but rugby. I left the interview with a firm handshake and a feeling of bemusement, unaware if I'd made the right impression or not. That afternoon I received another phone call informing me I had been successful. I'm glad I never told my Wigan loving interviewer that I prefer St Helens. Working in an office is a world away from the male dominated environment of a rugby club but I have to say, I enjoyed it. After a few months in the job, I was offered the position of team leader. Basically, I attended daily meetings, and took any queries from my team to the management and updated the board's daily performance indicator. I could delve into the daily workings of a tax office further but I won't, and it's not because I fear I may lose you in the complications of explaining the complex process involved, it's just that it's bloody boring. The most entertaining part of working in a tax office was the emails. I don't mean the business related, 'you saved the government 8p last year by not photocopying your arse at the Christmas party', nonsense. I mean the emails sent between friends. Myself, James Graham, Luke Rimmer, Karl Talent and Graham had an undercover football quiz going on every evening. We did enough work to reach the Key Performance Indicator, which basically meant you covered the minimum number of cases you had to do each night. Once this quota was met, it was football email time. We even started a tax office five-a-side football team. Every Wednesday before work we would play. The standard was not too bad considering that between the ten of us the body weight would be considered too much to enter a lift designed for twenty people. I'd formed a formidable defensive partnership with James, looking back, we must have been the only five a side team who played with a flat back four! Typically my enjoyment was short-lived as I broke my ankle whilst being out jumped by the smallest boy on the pitch and landing awkwardly. I did gain a tremendous amount of man points however by still going into work that evening, before finally admitting the pain was unbearable and taking myself to my second home, the hospital. X-rays confirmed that I had broken the Talus bone in the ankle and I was put in a protective cast. I would be out for even longer this time, indefinitely, in fact. I decided that I had sustained too many injuries to risk any further damage to myself, or risk injuries that could disrupt my job so I decided I could now announce what I'd known in my head for a while, I would retire from rugby altogether. This new low was another beginning in my battles with my weight. Though it was my decision to finish playing rugby, I was struggling to have to adapt to training alone. I can't describe how difficult it is to go from competitive sport every week, to having no challenges at all. Since I can remember, I have been trained, someone training me, telling me what to do. Once you finish competitive sport, you are on your own. My issue isn't training. I enjoy that side. I just get frustrated that all my efforts, the sweat, the dedication, pushing yourself, telling yourself that you won't be beaten no matter what. But that's it, there is nobody to beat, nobody is challenging you. It's just you against you and I have struggled to adapt to that. My life had revolved around the Saturday afternoon game for most of my life, now I was just another glorified pencil pusher. It's a hard role to have to adapt too. Now the biggest battle I face is with me, in my own head. I had met some good people in the tax office, different to what I was used to associating with in the past but nice all the same. Of the ones mentioned earlier, Luke is now an airline pilot for EasyJet, James still works at the tax office and is still the biggest Liverpool supporter I know. He religiously goes to home and away games, as well as attending any function to do with the club. James is a genuinely lovely person. I have since lost contact with Paul and Graham. Karl still works in the tax office and will forever be immortalised in the story below.

In 2012 it had been arranged with my friends back in Wales that a trip away was required. Amsterdam was the chosen destination and to be honest, I forget why this city was chosen for a boys weekend away over somewhere like Rome or Paris but it was. I think the thought of visiting Anne Frank's house or a trip on the famous canals swayed us. Culture is what we desired. The arrangements were made but late withdrawals left us two men down. I mentioned it in work to two boys on my team, Karl and Paul. They agreed to come. I had briefed them on the enormity of meeting my friends; I warned them that they were not normal. This was highlighted by the fact that my Welsh friends had sent me pictures of the journey up in the car, of them shooting each other at point blank range with a BB gun. Unperturbed by this, the weekend was confirmed. Four of my friends made the long journey up, Michael Mulhern, Taylor Jew-nose, one of the twins, either Phil or Steve, I say one of the twins because after all these years I can't tell them apart. They both look the same to me and who I thought would be Paul Boden. We were due to fly from Liverpool on the Friday morning. On the day of travelling, I had gone to collect my unhinged Welsh friends from their apartment, which they had booked for the night. I was greeted by a scene of total carnage, though, much to my delight and surprise, Adam Cardy was a last minute inclusion after Boden had dropped out. I enquired what had had happened as when I had spoken to them last night, they were leaving the pub and making their way to the apartment, ready for the early start in the morning. It turns out that the boys had unknowingly, on the way back, stumbled into another establishment that turned out to be a strip club, it's an easy mistake to make, and furthermore, they also struggled to find their way out so much, that they had no other options other than to stay until closing time. Adam practically spent his entire holiday money on every female dancer. He even dipped in to his monthly mortgage fund in order to obtain the wonderful services on offer.

Upon arriving in Amsterdam, we took a taxi to the city centre. While walking to our destination we were surprised to be approached and offered little packets of white powder by an exotic looking man. The cost of this apparent, small bag of Persil seemed extortionate, so we moved on. We continued to our hostel, amazed that the natives can afford to wash their clothes at those prices. We checked into our hostel and decided an afternoon snack was required. We settled on a small coffee shop which attracted us with its unusual sweet smell which emitted from the premises. The venue appeared to be strictly for heavy smokers, as every person had a large cigarette in their mouths. After studying the menu, I settled for the unusually named, Space Cake. After one bite, Adam ordered me to, "Take your time, it's not your lunch man, its hard-core drugs." Unbeknown to me, I had ordered a cake, laced with Cannabis. I was on holiday so finished my meal. Something funny must have been said because we spent the whole afternoon laughing and also nibbling on snacks. The evening was spent drinking Jägermeister, eating tasty cakes and seeing the sites of Amsterdam. We even went to watch a production in the local theatre, where we were surprised to find a couple making love on the stage; you won't get that in the Royal Palladium. When back in the room, my friend from work, Karl, informed me he intended to get the next flight home as he was concerned for his life if he stayed. I managed to convince him to stay; he's never been the same since. The next few days followed the same pattern, with one member having an unhealthy obsession with purchasing electronic devices that resembled the male anatomy; he must have visited, and bought a device, in every single shop in town. Amsterdam is a beautiful city, but there must have been some local policy that we were unaware of that meant you could only stay in a bar for a maximum of one drink, as every time we ordered a beverage and settled at our table we were soon approached and told by the manager, "Finish these, then leave, do not come back." My work colleague Karl was now known to the group as 'Ghost' as he didn't say a great deal and just blended mysteriously into the background. It appeared he was on the verge of a mental breakdown and our suspicions were backed up when the quietest member of the group got up to go to the toilet but not before walking past a pool table where two large, Hells Angel biker types, with full sleeve tattoos, long beards and chewing tobacco, were playing. As he walked past, he casually picked up the white ball as one of them was about to take a shot, and placed it down the hole. Karl, almost elegantly, walked off. It epitomized coolness and rendered our biker friends speechless. We made a hasty exit as to not get our heads smashed in when they came to their senses. Back at the hostel, we were joined by a gentleman from Switzerland, as the room was an eight man dormitory and there were only seven of us booked in. I imagine the sight of seven pissed up Brits is as welcoming as when General George Custer saw the Indians coming around the corner at the battle of Little Big Horn. In the early hours, Adam, heavily under the influence, greeted our foreign room-mate at the door in his baggy underpants and instructed him to 'get out you lairy cunt'. After some explaining, it was confirmed that Peter, was indeed in the right room. Peter was inundated with questions that you only get to ask when you meet somebody from a different country and as we are due to leave the European Union, we felt it would be a good time to ask the important questions, such as, can you yodel? Do you like Toblerones? Have you got a Swiss army knife? And are the cuckoos in a cuckoo clock real? All perfectly valid questions we thought. In the midst of the excitement, Michael Mulhern fell off the top bunk. The final night's highlight was Paul returning home after going missing for half the night. We were so concerned about our friend's whereabouts that at one stage, somebody suggested getting out of bed to go and look for him. It was decided that

'Amsterdam has him now' so we thought better of it. Paul did indeed return with his two front teeth missing and badly cut face. He explained he was set upon by three men as he walked along the canal. But evidence suggests the injuries were in fact caused by a transgender dwarf wearing a nappy, who Paul had laughed at earlier in the night. We all saw the funny side of it, even if Paul did not. We returned home, the magnificent seven, triumphant that we had conquered Amsterdam. We agreed to make the trip an annual event, to celebrate our glory. I can report that in the five years since the first trip to Amsterdam, we have never been back as a group since. I felt compelled to write that story in a ridiculous far-fetched manner, because it seems unbelievable but in reality, it was all true. It was one of those weekends where everything fell into place; good friends, great stories and great memories.

I returned to Amsterdam the following year, not with a group this time, just with Adam. Unbeknown to us and this is no way an excuse, but the weekend we picked happened to be the same weekend as the world's biggest Gay Pride Festival. A fellow passenger on the flight over even commented that we made a lovely couple. The second trip was spent pretty much the same as the first, in the coffee shops. Having spent the first day on the Space Cakes, I literally got Dutch courage and decided to upgrade to a joint. I ordered the strongest joint available, after I confirmed to the shop owner that I was indeed a regular smoker and could handle its potency. In reality, I tried cigarettes when I was a kid and hated it. Here I was twenty years later, about to smoke some pure Moroccan Hash. I'm such a novice that this supposed hard-core smoker had to ask the owner to roll it for me. I sat down and took my first drag; it didn't seem that bad, what was all the fuss about? Half an hour later and my entire body felt like it was in a bubble with everything passing by really slowly. Adam was right next to me but I had to keep checking every thirty seconds if he was still there. It felt like hours since I had last seen him. We sat outside the pub and marvelled at the size of a tree nearby. To us, it looked over a hundred feet, stretching high into the sky above. The next day we walked past it, sober and above all, not under the influence of the Moroccan hash, it was little more than a twig.

Whilst there, we decided to sample a few other things we had missed the first time around, namely, magic mushrooms. We purchased the fungi delicacy and proceeded to our room. My initial reaction was one of disappointment. I should have known better than to jump to conclusions. At first, I didn't feel a bloody thing. I wasn't expecting an out of body experience but for the ten euros that I paid, I expected a tingling at least. I'd been lying on my bed for around an hour, I couldn't sleep due to the heat. I got up to use the bathroom and suddenly it hit me. The floor had turned into a water bed; I couldn't stand up for fear of falling over. I crawled my way to the bathroom to relieve myself. What followed were the most bizarre few moments of my life. Upon urinating, I turned to the sink to wash my hands. I noticed my reflection in the bathroom mirror and I suddenly couldn't remember if I had actually had a piss not ten seconds before. I attempted the deed again and was satisfied that I had. I turned to the sink, caught sight of myself in the mirror and the same process started again. This was ridiculous. In an attempt to trick myself, I attempted to pee once more and was again unsuccessful but this time I decided to leave my penis out as to prove that I had finished. I paused for a few moments before Looking down. I seemed to remember my plan. I turned to leave then thought, wait a minute, is my penis hanging out because I need a wee, or because I've just had a wee? I couldn't take this anymore, as I was increasingly freaking out. I opened the bathroom door and did what any other normal person would do; I stood there, with my penis in my hand and announced to Adam that I'd forgotten how to piss and that he needed to watch me to allay my fears.

The answer was a resounding 'Fuck off you pervert'. Frustrated; I crawled back along the water bed floor and into bed. I never did get to the bottom of it. Now I should point out, for the record, that I am certainly not a user of drugs, but while in Amsterdam, it would indeed be rude not to.

(Above) Amsterdam. Buller, Adam and Me

'Life through the lens'

(Above) Amsterdam. Me, Adam and three random people

(Below) Me and my Dad. Tenerife. 1997

(Above) The Beatles. Waterloo Karaoke. 2007

(Below) Me and South African Dave. 2007

(Above) Waterloo rugby club BBQ. 2007

(Below) Me looking impressed. Late 80's

(Above) Taibach rugby club tour to Liverpool 2008

(Above)_Alun Thomas's stag day out In Cardiff dressed as WWF wrestlers

(Above) Painting the Waterloo flat with Dan Hall, Bruno and Dave Yorke

(Below) The Infamous arse of Bruno

141

(Above) Waterloo Rfc heading over to Ireland for a match 2007

(Below) Grand hotel, Port Talbot to watch Wales in the semi final at Euro 2016

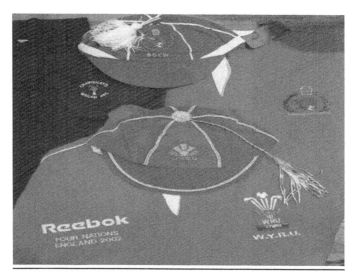

(Above) A collection of Welsh international caps and jerseys 1999-2004

(Below) Taibach u'16s after winning the district cup against Measteg 1999

(Above) Taibach tour to Liverpool. 2008

(Below) Me and Yorkie. Waterloo rugby club 2007.

(Above) Amsterdam square. Karl (Ghost) in background.

(Below) Rock 'n' roll star. 2010

(Above) Afan Lido football club. Treble winners. 1998.

(Below) Players night out. Walkabout, Liverpool. 2008

(Above) modelling the waterloo Rugby shirt. 2007

(Below) Fancy dress. Dyers, Hibbard, Me and Dan Williams. Xmas eve 2006

Chapter Eleven

'The death of you and me...'

In my early teens, I didn't have much time for girls. If I was invited to a house party I would be too busy training. Back then there wasn't the social media dominated society you have today where people you know are all linked under Facebook. It wasn't the case it is today of simply sending a personal message. If you liked someone, you had to take the time to talk to them, ask them for their landline number, and then pluck up the courage and run the gauntlet of phoning and hoping her dad didn't answer and having to explain yourself as to why you are calling his daughter in the first place. Luckily for me, I completely avoided this process because I was happy going out with my mates. I didn't want or have time for a girlfriend. Though it would be naive for me to make out like I was an amateur monk in my youth; I was young, reasonably handsome, had my own teeth and was confident. I'd had one or two girlfriends in my later teens; one was during my last year at school. We got together after she sent me a Christmas card saying 'to Matt, the rugby player' and I sent one back simply to 'The dancer.' I suppose this was the old fashioned way of flirting. But it worked. My other relationship was when I was 17; to a girl from Cymmer in the valleys above Port Talbot. It was only about five miles from my parents' home but the weather could be completely different up there. I'd gone to see her one afternoon just before Christmas. I'd left Port Talbot earlier that day; it was cold but certainly not frosty. I'd only been there a couple of hours but I had to get home for rugby training that evening. As I said my goodbyes I opened the door and was confronted with at least a foot of snow. I couldn't believe it, where the fuck did all that come from? Still, I decided to attempt to get back home. I drove out of the village and it was a beautiful sight seeing the Welsh mountains covered in flawless white snow. It was like a scene from a fairy tale. Further down the road and the snow became less and less until, eventually, there was not even a flake to be seen. I increased my speed; I'd taken this route a few times so knew of the sharp bends up ahead.   I was listening to the rock band, Queen's song: 'We Are the Champions. As I turned into the bend, I must have hit black ice as the cars back end spun out. I'll always remember this, as prior to hitting the ice I was really belting the song out. Just as Freddie sings, "We are the champions, of the wooooorld," the car began to spin out. I, for some reason, continued to sing. I followed Freddie Mercury's lead by singing "We are the champions of the....." but in my terrified state I replaced the word 'world' for the more appropriately elongated version of the word 'shiiiit.' I held this note perfectly until the car was under control again. Either side of me were potentially deadly hazards; to my left were the mountain walls and to my right was a sheer drop of about two hundred feet, with only a small barrier to stop any vehicle unfortunate enough to go into it. I couldn't get the car back under control and so I continued to spin. It must have only lasted five or six seconds but it felt like an hour. Miraculously, I somehow managed to avoid any contact with either the wall or the barrier. The danger wasn't over there; I had come to a stand still on the wrong side of the road. I was frozen in terror. I looked up and saw a car hurtling towards me. I braced for impact, but again, somehow, the driver managed to swerve at the last minute, completely avoiding me. I checked myself to make sure I wasn't in fact dead and once confirmed I went back to singing my song and carried on in a state of shock. How lucky was I? Bloody hell! Both relationships seemed like the real thing when you are that age but looking back, they were nothing serious as they both lasted no more than a few months at best.

Shortly before moving to Liverpool, I met a girl who I did like at the time named Natalie. I'd met her on a night out in Port Talbot and we got on well. I should add that I was on a night out with another girl I was seeing at the time and Natalie was her friend from school. For months after, we'd meet up, late at night and would exchange messages. We had to be secretive as she already had a boyfriend. My friends tried to warn me that this type of relationship could end in disaster, for both of us, but I told them not to worry as she intended on breaking up with him to be with me. The longer I had to keep this secret, the harder it got not to tell anyone. I happened to mention to the sister of a friend one evening that I was seeing someone, after being asked why I was single. Unbeknown to me, the girl I was confiding in also happened to know Natalie's boyfriend. She went on to tell him everything. I received a text message in work the next day, Natalie hit the roof and her exact words to me were, 'get the fuck out of my life.' This completely hit me for six. Suddenly I became the bad guy. I was young and naïve; I didn't have a bad bone in me. I was told it was over between them, or at least, things would be over between them. I hadn't and wouldn't mention it to purposely break them up, I wasn't like that.

Obviously their relationship wasn't over in her eyes and after Natalie's outburst it seemed apparent she still cared for her boyfriend far more than she was telling me. I felt I had been strung along and I wasn't prepared to wait forever. I felt confused as to what had happened in the previous months and to be honest, I felt a bit of a dick. I didn't know which way to turn. As luck would have it, a few days later I had the phone call to offer me the chance to play for Waterloo. I think this rejection helped in my decision to move to Liverpool. Less than a month after this incident, I was off. It was in Liverpool where my first serious relationship began. One of the boys in the rugby team had started seeing a local girl, who in turn, brought her friends to watch the games. I met Gemma in the bar after the game, she seemed nice enough and we got on quite well. As was the usual order of the night, we would all go into the local village for drinks. This became a weekly ritual and eventually we arranged to meet up for a date. We didn't really have much in common except we both liked our nights out at the time but that relationship suited me. I trained most nights and played on Saturdays so I only ever saw her after the game. After a few months, I was told I had to leave the rugby flat I was living in as it was only a short term agreement that I could stay there. Gemma lived at home with her parents. Neither of us could afford a place on our own so we took the impractical step of moving in together. I don't think either of us considered our relationship to be that serious but as we both needed to move out and as we got on, it seemed like a good idea. I was fortunate that David Morris had recently finished renovating a flat in the Blundellsands area, a short walk to Waterloo Rugby Club. He passed my name on to the landlord, a price was agreed and we moved in. Shortly after, we were travelling back to the flat after visiting Gemma's parents. As we drove along the main road, heading into Crosby, we stopped at traffic lights, opposite the Liver pub hotel. We noticed a commotion ahead in the opposite lane involving an Audi and a red transit van. We thought nothing of it really and Road rage isn't that uncommon in Liverpool. We then heard loud bangs which sounded like gun fire and a car drove off. It sped past us at a ridiculous speed, going through the red light in the process. We watched as the car then performed a U-turn in the petrol station and came back our way. It stopped alongside the driver's side of the van. A man got out of the speeding car and fired three or four shots at the person in the driver's seat. By now drinkers in the nearby pub had come out to see what all the noise was. The gunmen casually reloaded and shot the driver a final time before getting in the car and

153

speeding off again. We had just witnessed an execution. It was surreal. The driver's girlfriend was in the middle of the road screaming but there was nothing she could do. The man was already dead. People rushed to console the girl, who by now was understandably hysterical. Somebody placed a coat over the victim and the police were called. They later found the assassin's car burnt out, a short drive from where the crime took place. It turned out it was a gangland execution over an unpaid debt involving drugs. It's scary to think how little a life can matter to somebody to do such a thing but, at the same time, I suppose that is the chance you take when you associate yourself in that environment. By now, Gemma and I were settled into the flat and as in all relationships, the early days were fine. Nobody enters into a relationship unless they want to and at the time, I was happy with how things were going. There were some good times, having no commitments, we were able to travel a lot more and visited some nice places. I preferred to visit cities, Gemma preferred beach holidays. It's a compromise you take in the early days. I had built up a good relationship with her brother Tom. Tom was the same age as me and we shared similar interests. We attended music concerts together. One particular gig was in Manchester University to watch Liam Gallagher's new band, Beady Eye. We spent the afternoon drinking and made our way to the venue and anticipated a good performance. The venue was small, cramped and extremely warm. We spent the majority of the concert jumping up and down. I had mentioned to Tom that the heat was unbearable and by now, the sweat was dripping off me. Towards the end of the show, an Oasis classic named 'Rock 'n' Roll Star' was played. The crowd went wild, as did I. I remember bouncing up and down like a child on a pogo stick and next thing, wham. I woke up outside on the wall. The heat and all day drinking had caused me to collapse. I had been dragged outside, luckily before being trampled by the thousands in attendance. I didn't remember a thing. Tom was next to me complaining that he had lost not only his mobile phone but also his glasses. I found it quite amusing until I realized I was missing a shoe and my jeans were badly ripped. By now we both felt sorry for ourselves and so went to get the last train home. The sight of me wearing only one shoe and my ripped jeans revealing my left arse cheek raised a few eyebrows from fellow passengers, but all in all, it was a great night. The times Gemma and I spent at the flat would be arguably better than the time we would eventually would spent in the house. In 2010 we bought a house in the Merseyside area of Litherland. I had finished my rugby career and had just begun working for the HMRC. I was looking forward to the next chapter of my life. I took, what turned out to be, the disastrous decision to propose to Gemma, with no explanation other than it felt right at the time. Hindsight is a marvellous thing and anyway, she agreed. I had booked a surprise holiday for the next morning on the assumption of Gemma agreeing to marry me. We were due to travel to Paris the next day at 8am. Gemma's brother, Tom, arranged a few drinks in town as celebration. I informed him it wouldn't be the usual drinking binge as I was due to travel shortly. We took the sensible option, as we always did, of attempting to consume every short on the menu. From Absinthe, to Jägermeister to whisky, we drank the lot. A few hours later I somewhat, sensibly decided against Tom's suggestion of going on to a nightclub to see his friends. I obviously had some of my wits about me so we went our separate ways. I called into the Burger King for something to eat, before heading to the train station. I was in good spirits as I approached the barriers. The guard asked for my ticket which I showed him. As I entered the platform, the same guard stopped me from boarding my train as I was deemed too drunk. I protested my innocence and upon hearing this commotion, the transport police got involved. After a brief exchange, in which I'll admit to swearing, I was jabbed in the back with a truncheon and had my Burger King thrown on the floor. I was arrested for being drunk and disorderly. I was taken to the police station and was thrown in a cell, again. I informed them that I had got engaged that evening and was due to go to Paris, by now, in six hours time. A short time later I was taken down to have my picture and fingerprints taken. I also asked to be breathalysed. I was only just over the drink drive limit. Even the policeman suggested I couldn't have been that drunk in the first place. I agreed. At 6am, I was cautioned and released. Gemma was waiting outside the station for me. She had packed my bags and we went straight to the airport. Looking back, I wished I had taken my packed bags and gone alone. In complete silence we drove to Manchester. Not the best of starts to potential married life. Once in Paris, the argument intensified. I pleaded my innocence but Gemma was having none of it. I left the room and walked the streets of Paris on my own. I visited all the attractions and covered nearly twelve miles that evening. I eventually returned in the early hours. We made up but we were ignoring the warning signs.

After a few years and mindful of the issue with my kidney, I wanted to settle down. I no longer enjoyed wild nights out, I wanted quiet nights in. this caused massive conflict as I was constantly accused of being boring and told 'you only live once.' This phrase, above all others, really pisses me off. Most weekends, Gemma would still go out with her friends, but with going out came the trip to the hairdressers, nail salon, new dress and usually a private booth with an expensive drinks package in some pretentious bar. She would spend a fortune. I didn't mind at the beginning, she worked, it was her money. Plus it gave me a bit of time to myself. That said, due to our planned wedding, my bank account was checked on a daily basis. Gemma had access to my statements and would highlight particular transactions and question them. I treated myself to a bottle of aftershave one time. The next day Gemma hit the roof, suggesting we get a joint account because it's the only way she could manage my spending. I felt like a child being dictated to. I felt like the old me had gone, that I'd given up and settled for something that I knew I didn't really want. I felt I had no way out. When you're lying in bed alone in the early hours dreading your future wife to be coming through the door, you know your relationship is finished. I'm a loyal person and fear of hurting her kept me there for longer than I should have. It was unfair to her and unfair to me. A number of times after an argument, I got in my car and started to drive home to Wales. I intended to stay there for good. Every time, I turned the car around and headed back, I felt another chance had gone. In the end we were blatantly horrible to each other. In front of family and friends, we, of course, put on a smile and lapped up the attention for our future wedding. I would be asked for ideas on the venue, suits and flower arrangements. I didn't really comment because by then, I couldn't really give a shit. I had no real intention of going through with it.

I was growing increasingly frustrated at home and I needed to release some pressure. Even though I was now overweight and certainly not match fit, I decided to play rugby and make an appearance for the Waterloo seconds team. The game itself wasn't actually that bad, we were winning comfortably and I was enjoying it despite blowing out of my arse. It's no excuse but the frustrations of my home life at the time must have had an impact on what happened next. Towards the end of the game, a player on the opposite team made a break and was heading for the try line. I chased him back and made a good tackle. I also got to my feet and won the ball, however, the ref awarded a penalty against me. I was livid. It doesn't matter to me if I'm playing for my country or playing second team rugby in an empty field, I want to win. I aggressively asked what the penalty was for. The ref responded by showing me a yellow card. This was absolute bollocks. I turned to walk away, calling the ref a prick as I left. I heard the loud shrill of his whistle and him ordering me back. I turned around and he was stood about twenty feet away from me, ordering me to come to him, pointing to the floor below him. He then stood with his hands behind his back, refusing for the game to restart unless I came over to stand at his feet. I hated these types of power hungry refs. I slowly strolled over and he produced a red card and in a patronising way, waved it in my face. I completely saw red, literally. I pushed the ref and made some abusive comments. I had to be dragged away as I threatened to see him after the game. The red mist had come down and my head had completely gone. Back in the changing rooms, I punched the wall, repeatedly; I wished it was the referees head. I went home feeling a whole lot worse, the bloody game was supposed to be a stress reliever. My sending off and behaviour was reported and I was told to attend a hearing at the English RFU headquarters. I had no intention of going; I was retired officially, so didn't give a toss about the punishment. A Waterloo official attended the hearing in my absence. He told the hearing that apart from this outburst, I had an exemplary disciplinary record and had represented my country a few years previous. The panel handed me an eight month ban from the game. It could easily have been a few years, or even life. Abusing the officials is considered extremely serious, and rightly so. At the time I felt justified in my actions but looking back, I was completely out of order and embarrassed myself that day. I should have known better. Back at home, I was still unhappy. I was adamant in my head that the wedding would never happen. It sounds evil but actually going ahead with it seemed worse to me. I'm not a bad person, I don't like to see people upset, plus I didn't know how to tell her it was over. It made it worse that I was close to her family; they had been good to me since I met Gemma. We had been on family holidays, weekends in caravans and always spent Christmas in each others houses, not to mention they were a big help in doing the house up. In a strange way, I felt like I was letting them down more than anything. In the end, I took a cowardly way out. I'd been talking to a girl from work, we did get on but I had absolutely no attraction to her, let alone an interest in her. I used these conversations to say how unhappy I was at home. I mentioned I was trying to find the way to end it. One evening, I purposely left the laptop open, knowing that Gemma was due home soon. I intended for Gemma to see those messages. I heard her come home. I waited upstairs. I was unsure what her reaction would be. What if she doesn't read them? Those few minutes felt like hours. It wasn't long before she stormed up the stairs and threw the engagement ring at me. She didn't even say a word. My overriding emotion was relief. I didn't feel sad, just relief. If I'd done this prove to myself that it was definitely over then I was justified. The next few days proved difficult, her family, whom lived a few doors away, made passing comments, which maybe I deserved. Looking back, I probably did. I do feel a sense of remorse in the way I ended it but in reality, is there a good way to end a relationship? It had its desired effect, and for that, I was happy. In the aftermath, I decided to move out, it was my house, but I moved out. I later signed the house over to Gemma. For all my hard work and expense paid, I didn't receive a penny for it. I don't look back on these years with regret. I was a different person at the end of the relationship to the person I was when we first met. We just weren't compatible anymore. People change, it happens. Initially it was hard, not because I was sad about the break up but because I was alone. I had nobody to turn to really. My parents and friends were at the end of the phone but that's not the same. I worked as much as I could and I even contemplated returning to Wales and I probably would have, had it not been for the job I was due to start in the following month after the break up.

Chapter Twelve

'Every new beginning, comes from some other beginnings end....'

After the breakup, I checked myself into the Travel Lodge, on the Strand Road, Liverpool city centre. I had a few black bin bags and my rugby holdall, containing all my worldly possessions. I'd just started a new job working for the Home Office, in the immigration department. I had seen the job advertised on the civil service website while I was at the HMRC. I applied and was delighted to be offered the interview. I was sure I had blown it at the very first question because the interviewer asked me about leading on equality and diversity. Bloody hell, who starts an interview with a question like that? Couldn't he have asked me about rugby league teams like in my last interview? I must have stared at him for a minute. The little hamster going around in his wheel in my head was offering me nothing. I thought back to my time at the HMRC and remembered a girl who was once fasting due to Ramadan. I made some story up about the whole team supporting her and asking her questions as to why this is a celebrated month in the Islamic religion, so we could understand more about other faiths and why it is important to respect other beliefs. It worked, the answer scored highly. In reality, while she was fasting, the boys and I were having a Big Mac and chips at our desks. I later learned that all my subsequent answers had also scored highly so I was offered the position and given a start date for my new job. Besides being effectively homeless by this time, I saw it as a brand new start, again. Staying in the hotel was already costing a fortune, so I was glad when I had to go to Croydon for a few weeks as part of my training. All the hotels, food and transport would be paid for. It was a massive weight off my shoulders. I spent two weeks in Croydon, at the five star Croydon Park Hotel. It was a beautiful establishment, very grand. I'd developed a routine of visiting the gym, then relaxing in the sauna before heading out for an evening meal. It was all on company expenses so it felt like a holiday. It was just the break I needed after the previous months.

The time off also gave me a chance to find somewhere else to live, as I couldn't stay in the

Travel Lodge forever and it was embarrassing when on your first day at work you're giving a hotel as your main address. I'd seen a few properties online and things were taking shape again. When I arrived back in Liverpool, I arranged to view a flat down the waterfront, near the Pier Head. I fell in love with it straight away. It was modern, furnished, had views over the Mersey River and above all, it was mine. The fees for such a property were high but luckily my parents helped out with the deposit. The first few weeks were difficult; I had no television, no internet and no contact with anybody. I would sit and read books or would walk until the early hours taking in the sites I'd neglected to see since I arrived in Liverpool. It was refreshing. I bought myself a small fish tank and a Siamese fighting fish to go with it. I'd read that this particular fish prefers to live its life alone. It seemed to fit the same lifestyle that I was currently in so we both had a mutual existence, alone. I used this time to get fit. I still had issues with my weight so I would visit the gym twice a day. I began eating healthier and the weight soon dropped of me. I started to feel good again. I even contemplated a return to rugby. Work was also going well, I enjoyed the job and it was interesting. Part of my training would eventually take me to glamorous locations such as Croydon, Cardiff and Glasgow. Whilst in Glasgow, I was actually harassed and chased by a dwarf. I swear you couldn't make half of these stories up. I had been walking down the street when the little person approached me and asked me for some money. Instead of ignoring her, I kindly told her I had no change. She continued to follow me down the street for a good hundred metres. The Glasgow accent can be very strong and I had no idea what she was on about. In the end I had to tell her to fuck off. She responded by attempting to kick me. Her highest kick caught me just on the top of my ankle. I laughed it off and took refuge in a pub. The dwarf had only followed me in; I was being stalked by an angry elf, great. I hid in the toilet for a few minutes, satisfied that she would have given up the chase by now. I safely emerged. I looked around and was happy that I couldn't see her. I even checked under the tables, just in case. As I approached the entrance, I caught sight of a pair of eyes, straining to see over the usually waist high window. I couldn't believe it. She was relentless. I took my chances and headed for the door. I was confident that my strides would be considerably longer than hers. It would be like a pug trying to keep up with a horse. My plan worked, I glanced over my shoulder and was delighted to see that Grumpy had vanished. I wish I knew Snow White to inform her of her mate's behaviour.

Back at the Home Office, I had a good working relationship with a few of the boys there. One in particular, Cribby, suggested joining a dating site as I had mentioned to him of my boredom at being home alone every night. I insisted I had no intentions of getting into a relationship just yet, but he persuaded me by saying it's a good way to just meet new friends, just exchange numbers and chat. To be honest I liked the idea of being able to chat to people of a night. I didn't care about meeting, so I signed up. I immediately encountered a problem. Every time I was prompted to enter a username, the one I entered was already in use. I tried three or four separate names but to no avail. I was on the point of giving up when in frustration; I typed, 'Funky Spunk Monkey.' Typically, it was accepted, with no way of changing it. I did try immediately to amend this but it was proving a fruitless exercise so I just thought 'fuck it,' besides, I was amazed that nobody else had taken such a common name. And so, in the hunt to find a potential life partner, my future lover would know me as, Funky Spunk Monkey. Great! As is common with this method of meeting new people, it certainly threw up some interesting characters. I put it down to the username. One that springs to mind was a lady who lived nearby. She suggested going for a few drinks, to which I agreed. We met, and for me there was no physical attraction. The evening was fine, small talk, the usual life story. When suddenly she turned and asked me was I into bondage? I was taken aback by this and muttered, "Err not really." Ignoring my reply, the lady got really excited, tapping her knees while bouncing on the spot. She insisted I should try it. She asked me, "Have you ever used a strap on?" I informed her that I was aware of what it is but I had no need to use one, as my gender, the male, possess something a strap on is designed to replicate, namely, the penis. She laughed and explained that she would wear the strap on and use it on me. I felt foolish that I didn't catch on sooner. I'd been out of the dating game a while, maybe this was a normal request now? Now I am not homophobic but the very thought repulsed me. She gleefully told me that one of her previous boyfriends had the same trepidations as me but once he tried it, he loved it. After a bit of probing, not literally, it turned out her ex-boyfriend left her for another man. Not willing to take my chances on the same fate, I declined the tempting offer and wished her well in her future endeavours. Being the gentleman that I am, I walked my drunken lady friend safely home to her door. She was obviously horny; I came to this conclusion by remembering her proposition to insert objects into me. I don't mind admitting what I did next, I did what any man would do in that situation, I ran away, not looking back and once safely home I placed her number on the blocked list.

As a result of my encounter with the strap on loving nymphomaniac, I decided that online dating was most definitely not for me. I decided to revert back to the good old fashioned way, namely, standing at the bar in the hope that a female might talk to me. I attempted to delete my profile from the dating website but was met with a multitude of questions as to why I wanted to leave when there were five million singles ready to chat. I searched the options on offer and was disappointed to not see an option for 'leaving due to crazy bitch.' I decided that all things considered, I was happy enough on my own. It stayed that way for a whole week. I was in work one afternoon, we weren't supposed to use mobiles but as the afternoons were usually quiet, we were allowed to keep them on us in case of an emergency. I was aware that I had received a notification from the dating site that I had tried to delete a few days earlier. Without any hope or expectation, I opened the email. It simply read 'KatBomb' liked your profile. Kathryn will deny that she effectively made the first move but I can confirm this is indeed, true. I was curious as to who this mystery admirer could be. I clicked on her profile, and was amused to find her profile picture was blank. The girl with no face. I sarcastically sent her a message to compliment her on her picture and that I particularly liked her hair. They say that every great journey starts with a single step and this was no exception. A couple of messages were exchanged as I was immediately captivated by this mystery girl. My phone went from being kept in the locker at work, to being kept in my pocket at all times. I didn't care if I got in trouble, messaging this girl became my obsession. I'd received a picture of the girl with no face and I was immediately attracted to her. She was beautiful, she still is. We exchanged messages for what seemed like an eternity, getting to know each other. Some nights I'd fall asleep with my phone in my hand or whilst writing a reply. My obsession went as far as to waking up in the early hours, just to see if Kathryn had messaged. One day I told her that I'd prepared a compatibility questionnaire and if we didn't get similar results then we'd have no future together. Luckily for her, she did very well, getting nearly all of them correct. The question that nearly affected everything was Kathryn not liking milk, whereas, milk, is my favourite. I thought long and hard and decided I could overlook this issue. By now we were desperate to meet in person but finding a suitable day proved difficult as we both worked long hours and neither of us had a car at the time. After a few weeks, we finally arranged to meet. The day arrived and the clock in work seemed to be going backwards. I was expecting a message to say that Kathryn would have to cancel but it never came. There was no turning back now. I got home from work later than I'd planned. We'd arranged to meet outside the John Lewis store in the Liverpool ONE Shopping Centre. To calm my nerves, I had a glass of wine, which turned into two, then the whole bottle. I felt like a school kid. Here I was, a fully grown man actually petrified of meeting a girl. Kathryn messaged to say she was on her way, it was happening. I made the short walk from my apartment. It felt like I was in a daze; I had a thousand thoughts going 'round and 'round. What do I say? Will she like me in person? Do I go to give her a kiss? A hug? Or even shake her hand? Shake her hand? It wasn't a business meeting; she wouldn't be scrutinising my CV. My heart was pounding when I got to the meeting point. Kathryn was running late so I then started to panic about my stance when she arrived. Do I stand up straight? Or be cool and lean against the wall? Bloody hell, get a grip! What was I thinking? I scanned every single person as they came around the corner. I didn't need to worry about recognizing her, as I saw her coming through the crowd of people. She looked beautiful. Kathryn later mentioned that she had first seen a boy walking towards her smiling and that he looked like Harry Potter. Her first thought was that I looked nothing like the pictures I had sent. She was relieved that I was in fact standing behind him. I don't even recall what was said when we first met face to face. I was still in that daze. We walked back to mine for drinks. It was freezing, so I cuddled her tight into me. The evening was even better than I thought it would be. It was nice to just be able to get along with someone, not fake, no falseness. It was the perfect night. We drank wine and watched the ships below on the river. The following weeks just seemed to get better and better. We still talked for hours on the phone and days out were arranged. This period felt like bliss. We went on regular date nights to the cinema and to, what would become our favourite restaurant, Fazenda, in Exchange Flags Square, Liverpool. We even went on bike rides along the waterfront. It felt like a life I thought I'd lost had been found again. I was happy. It had been a long time since I could really say that.

Chapter Thirteen

'Life is what happens to you while you're busy making other plans

I had booked a short break to Barcelona for Kathryn and myself. This city above all is my favourite, with so many attractions to see, great weather all year round and even better food. The night before we left finally gave me the opportunity to meet Kathryn's parents. I cleaned the flat from top to bottom, hoping to make a good impression. Meeting the parents can be a nerve-wracking occasion but my nerves were soon calmed when I met them, as Colin and Carole are both lovely, easy going people and the night went really well. The early days of a relationship are always nice, learning new things about each other, sharing experiences and what better place to get to know somebody than Barcelona. We spent the time visiting all the attractions, going for food and sampling the cocktails on offer at the hotel. During the night, we would just wander around the beautiful city and just get lost together, or I should say, lost in each other. It was a lovely few days with a girl I had fallen head over heels for. We spent the remaining days of the summer together. We would go for evening strolls along the prom, listening to the church bells ringing and to watch the firework displays from the cruise liners departing the city, waving to the passengers as the song, 'Time to say goodbye' was played, before they finally disappeared up the Mersey and onto the next destination.

One afternoon, we booked an open top bus ride around Liverpool. Kathryn had lived in the city all her life and I'd been there for many years but it was still interesting to learn about the history of buildings and streets that you would otherwise pass everyday without thinking twice. Whilst on the bus, a bird decided to shit right next to us, covering Kathryn and I in the process. They say its good luck and it certainly was a sign of things to come. One memorable day happened in early July. We had decided to rent bikes and spend the late evening enjoying the sun. We rode along the prom. It was like a scene from a love film, riding in and out of people, ringing the bell as we went by and glancing at each other, constantly smiling, before getting off the bikes to watch the sunset. It was a simple day, nothing extravagant but it felt like something special was happening. My uplifted mood was soon brought crashing back down as It was around this time that I was given the sad news that my Uncle James had died from cancer. It did come as a shock as he had only been diagnosed a few weeks before. My parents were away at the time on holiday. My brother Mike had gone around to his house one morning and found him on the sofa, he had passed away through the night. My parents immediately returned home to make plans for the funeral. As I got older, I lost contact with James, though I would always receive a Christmas card and birthday card off him. I have fond memories of James. As a youngster I would go to his house and would watch films, usually the Tom Cruise classic, Top Gun. We would listen to music or play on his computer. I even had a junior tool kit and would make items in the shed with him. He was a massive fan of The Beatles and would play 'Yellow Submarine' on the stereo, whilst pretending the bed was the vessel. It's another memory from my time as an innocent child that I look back on and smile. The funeral was emotional, especially for my father, as he was now the last remaining family member from his childhood home. It was a great turn out, for a lovely man and some fantastic stories were told that showed how well thought of James was. When I returned to Liverpool, Kathryn was waiting for me at the train station. We went back to the flat to get ready for a meal, as it was her birthday. Before the meal, we had a booked a lane at the Hollywood bowling alley, on Edge Lane. We met up with Kathryn's parents, and for the first time, I met her younger brother, Isaac, her older sister, Fran and her boyfriend, Ste. It was a lovely evening and ended with me staying over at Kathryn's house for the first time. A couple of weeks later, Kathryn messaged that she needed to see me. When she arrived, she sat me down and told me she had something to tell me. As with most people, hearing these words, it set off a multitude of scenarios in your mind. I was neither prepared, or have never been so shocked, excited, terrified, delighted in all my life upon hearing the words, "I'm pregnant." I ran to the nearest Boots chemist to purchase multiple pregnancy test kits to be sure. Every single test confirmed that Kathryn was indeed pregnant. Initial delight was replaced by concern and the realization that we were hardly in the position to raise a tiny human being. Our concern was that we had only been together a short time. No doubt we were in love but there was still a lot to learn about each other. We felt that if we had a baby now, we would miss out on all the exciting things that new couples do. Holidays abroad, nights out, moving in together, however, once we had got over the initial shock, our worries returned to excitement. Our families and friends were informed of the pregnancy and the countdown was on. The next few weeks were filled with morning sickness, browsing the internet for baby manuals and discussing who the baby would look like. Kathryn and I decided that we should move in together, as we had a lot of preparation ahead of us in the coming months. I handed in my notice in on my flat and another journey was about to take place. Kathryn lived in The Huyton area of Liverpool. She shared the house with her parents, who had recently moved in with Kathryn after returning from Scotland. It was great having her parents around because I was working more hours in an attempt to save some money for the imminent arrival of our baby. Also, having her parents around meant that Kathryn was not at home alone, this was a big relief to me. We had gone for the scan, adamant that we were having a little girl. This was mainly based on an old wives tale over the shape of the bump. Seeing your baby up on the monitor up on the screen is an amazing moment. It suddenly makes it all very real. We were delighted to learn that, what we thought was definitely a girl, was in fact, a little boy. As with all parents to be, we completely went overboard with clothes and other items. It's all part of the journey though. Moses basket, pram, cot, steriliser and bottles were all purchased. We were almost ready for an event in which ultimately you can never be fully prepared for. To pass the time, we had booked a beautiful cottage in Wales, high in the mountains overlooking Port Talbot. The journey down turned out to be a mini disaster, missing the turning off the M5 for South Wales, twice, and instead ending up in Coventry, twice. We eventually arrived, four hours late. We had called in to see my parents who had yet to meet the now six months pregnant, Kathryn. At the end of the evening I took Kathryn to sample the fine local cuisine on offer, rissole and chips. The next few days were lovely - walks down the beach, even though temperatures were in minus figures, cosy nights in the cottage and a full day at Margam Park. Exploring the castle and feeding ducks. We returned home and soon began to count down the days, not months. The due date had arrived, a week later and we were still waiting. In fact, it was nearly two weeks later when Kathryn first started getting initial labour pains. Two journeys were made to the hospital, one in the early hours of the morning that proved to be false a start, and again, the next morning. We arrived for an arranged appointment, Kathryn was assessed and a procedure given to hopefully start the labour. The waiting was unbearable, even Macy the dog was fed up with our pacing up and down. Finally the labour pains started for real. We travelled to the Women's Hospital in Liverpool. Upon arrival, Kathryn was taken in a wheelchair up to the maternity department. The pain was now so intense and as the contractions were only thirty seconds apart, Kathryn struggled to walk. It was definitely happening. It wouldn't be long before we'd, very shortly, be meeting our baby boy, or so we thought. We were taken into a side room and one of the nurses commented that she must have a high pain threshold as the contractions were very high on the monitor and so frequent with it. Kathryn's mother, Carole, and I felt helpless; all we could do was give encouragement. Into the early hours we went and still no change. A doctor was watching the monitors from his office; he was concerned about the frequency of the contractions and Kathryn was eventually told to have an epidural, though we were also told that we would have to wait as the doctor who administers it was currently at a different hospital. It was a long wait on just gas and air, with no let-up in the pain. The nurse kept coming in and informing us of the estimated time that the doctor would be back to give the epidural. Twice we reached the estimated time and twice we were told we had to wait a little bit longer. It was a frustrating night. Eventually, the next morning and sixteen hours since we first entered the hospital, we were taken down to the delivery suite. Finally an epidural would be given. It was heart-breaking to see someone you love in so much pain. Kathryn was getting upset that she couldn't get into a comfortable position for the doctor to insert the needle, as the she couldn't breathe on her left side due to the baby's feet being under her ribs. The procedure was eventually done and the nurse, who was fantastic, was able to assess Kathryn. She was not satisfied that Kathryn was dilated to the extent a previous nurse had advised and suggested we might need a C-section if things did not change in the next few hours. We had considered this option to be highly likely as my family genes tend to produce big babies that Kathryn's tiny child bearing hips would struggle with. A few hours later, the nurse again examined Kathryn. She advised us that she was not dilated at all so an emergency C-section was the only option. Kathryn had been in labour for two days now. We waited patiently, nervously, excited. After only a short time, Kathryn was taken down to theatre and I was told to wait in a side room before I would be called for. The nurse in charge came to collect me and asked if I had a camera to film the moment our baby arrived. It was a fantastic gesture. I entered the room and Kathryn was lying on the bed. She was exhausted, so was I and I hadn't been through anything in comparison. Kathryn was shaking uncontrollably due to the drugs given and also through tiredness and shock. The nurse asked me to pin Kathryn down to stop her from moving while the surgeon performed the caesarean. At 17:46 we heard our baby boy's cry for the first time. It's a wonderful sound. He was taken to be cleaned up before being brought over to us. As he was handed over to us by the nurse, he peed all over me and Kathryn. What a way to introduce yourself to your parents. I had never seen anything so beautifully perfect in my life. This tiny human being that we had created was like a work of art. Kathryn cried. It was over; I felt like crying as well but managed to keep it together. Kathryn had been fantastic from start to finish. I've never been as proud of someone as I was of Kathryn at that moment. Ethan Llewellyn Davies Bradley had arrived, weighing 8lb 15. That evening, I was not allowed to stay with Kathryn as she was taken to the new mothers ward. I hated saying my temporary goodbyes but Kathryn needed her rest. I drove home, dropping Carole off on the way. It had been a long few days for everybody. I walked through the front door where I saw all the congratulations cards, flowers and teddy bears and I'm not ashamed to say, I burst into tears. It had been an emotional rollercoaster. I don't think I slept at all that night. I was exhausted but now the realism and enormity of the next few months began to hit home. Still, I couldn't wait to get up in the morning and visit Kathryn and my baby boy.

Me and Ethan

(Above) Taking in the enormity of what's ahead

(Below) Kathryn and Ethan

Chapter Fourteen

'Beautiful Boy...'

The following morning, I went to meet my parents at their hotel for breakfast. They had come up the previous day but had been unable to see Kathryn due to there being a limit in the delivery room. I wasn't allowed to visit Kathryn until eleven that morning. I couldn't wait to see mother and baby. My baby. My son. It still sounded bizarre. Kathryn had sent me a picture of the two of them. They looked adorable. Ethan was born with thick black hair. I was envious. Once at the hospital, the nurse gave the baby a little bath before all the family arrived. Kathryn went to have a shower, along with her mother Carole. I was alone with Ethan for the first time. It really is terrifying seeing something so small, knowing that soon I would be responsible for bringing up this tiny human being, despite not knowing where to even start. I was enjoying the father-son moment when I suddenly heard a loud emergency alarm on the ward. It soon became clear that it was coming from the shower room Kathryn and her mother had just gone into. I panicked as the nurse rushed to attend. She emerged seconds later and told me not to worry; Carole had only leaned on the panic alarm. Talk about trying to scare me; my nerves were just holding out without that happening as well. We had booked a private room in the hospital, that way we had our own space. Our families came to visit and lots of messages of congratulations were sent and it started to feel real. I was still on a massive high and didn't want to come down. A few days later we were allowed bring Ethan home. Kathryn and I were alone for the first time with our baby. As I mentioned, it's a terrifying prospect. We'd had the guidance of the nurses, of our parents but now it was just the three of us. I think the parental instincts are stronger in women than they are in men, when it comes to new born babies at least. The thought of holding Ethan made me seize up immediately. My body became rigid and I would be afraid to move. Kathryn, on the other hand, took to it like she had been a mother all her life. The first few weeks were an enormous learning curve; you adapt your whole life around this tiny person. Everything was put in place long before the baby arrived; however, we had ordered a new sofa that was a month behind schedule. We were sat on garden chairs and bean bags, hardly suitable for a mother and child, let alone a woman who has just gone through an emergency C-section.

After a month, I was due back in work. I had already used up my paternity leave and annual leave. The thought of going back to work filled me with dread. It wasn't that I didn't enjoy the job, it was that I didn't want to leave Kathryn alone all day with the baby. She was still occasionally having emotional outburst and plus I didn't want to miss anything. The crawling, the rolling over, the smiles, I wanted to be there for it all. I decided to request that my working hours be cut to the minimum hours I could, which was thirty seven. Before that, I was working closer to fifty hours a week, this meant working most weekends. My request was rejected as I'd signed the contract, confirming I would work these hours, before the baby was born. I went to see my line manager, Mark, and hoped that if I explained that my decision was based on the fact that I had a new born baby at home and wanted to help out there as much as I could. Mark was a patronising prick and personally I couldn't stand him. His reply was simply, "That's what the mother's maternity leave is for." He had no children himself, probably because he was a self-centred idiot who thought work was everything. I informed him that I had no intention of working any more than five days a week before walking out of his office. It certainly raised tensions between us. Shortly after, a night out was arranged with work to watch the Champions League final. The night started off fine that was until my line manager Mark showed up. A few of the boys had got chatting to a hen party in the bar. Mark, as always, wanted to be the centre of attention. He wore a thick gold necklace and a matching bracelet. He looked like an overweight Mr. T but I didn't pity this fool. He started telling the girls that he was the manager and that I and the other boys had to do whatever he said. If we didn't, he could sack us on the spot. I ignored this comment as we moved on to the next bar. We had all had a few drinks when I decided to confront Mark as to why he would not let me reduce my hours. I knew it was probably a bad idea but up to this point in my life, I'd never done things logically, so why start now? Mark's reply to my question was simply, "Because I said so, that's why." I informed him that was not an answer. He went on to comment, quite dismissingly, "I'm your manager so I decide what hours you work." By now some of the others had overheard our argument and to be fair, backed me up. One of them said, "Be fair Mark. Matt's got a new-born baby; let him reduce his hours if he wants." Mark's reply infuriated me, "So what? I don't give a fuck." I saw red and went for him. I was in his face telling him we'll sort this out, outside. He shit himself, probably literally. I could see he didn't want to fight me. I'm not a bully so I didn't press the matter. I'd made my point and he just stood there like a frightened boy so I went outside alone to calm down. All the boys came out to see me; they all understood why I had gone for Mark. He was the one out of order. Things began to boil over and another argument broke out between Mark and one of the boys named Andy. There was a bit of pushing and shoving before Andy threw a punch. Mark made a sharp exit for a taxi and appeared to be close to tears. The following week in work, Mark was off with stress. When he returned he sent me an email to suggest a mediation session. Now, I'm not illiterate, but I thought he meant meditation, sitting in a darkened room with scented candles listening to whale music. I wondered what good that would do. I later learned mediating meant meeting to discuss the root of the problem. My issue was simple. It was him. I was increasingly despising going to work, I hated leaving Kathryn and the baby, especially if she had had a sleepless night and would then be expected to look after our baby all day. I was becoming irritable and volatile.

In work one day, one of the boys was pushing me for an answer as to why I wanted to reduce my hours, as I would be losing money. That's all people thought in that place, money, not work-life balance. I said nothing, I didn't want to talk about it, I knew he wouldn't understand anyway but he persisted.

He made a comment about me needing to sort myself out, and again I saw red. I threw a pile of trays across the room and lunged at him. He literally ran away, I don't blame him. We had a waiting room full of asylum applicants that saw the incident. I was restrained and told to have five minutes outside. I didn't need five minutes, I needed time off. The next few weeks I started taking more and more days off, unauthorized leave. I put it down to stress and anxiety. I even went to the doctors who prescribed me tablets. He said I could be depressed. Tablets are not my thing and I refused to take them. Anyway, I had rejected his diagnosis as I thought depression meant that I wanted to kill myself. Thankfully, I have never had these thoughts. I'm not one to express my feelings openly. I hide things well and bottle it up. That's not a bad reflection on those closest to me, I know I could approach them and be truthful with them and they would understand, but to me feeling useless and down is a weakness. This is something I have issues with, how I am perceived. For years I have been the happy, always smiling, do anything for anyone boy. As a result, I don't know how to be anything else. During this period, I felt the opposite of fine. It wasn't just me who noticed I wasn't myself. Kathryn had mentioned that I seemed to lack any motivation. She was right, I felt useless and everything was getting me down. Every time I held the baby he would cry, he stopped immediately when he went back to Kathryn. I didn't change a nappy, I didn't wash his clothes, I didn't make the food or do the dishes. I didn't do anything. I sat on the couch watching TV. Not really talking. I wanted to be invisible. I decided I needed to do something to get myself out of this rut. We agreed that the job situation was obviously bringing me down. I wanted to leave. The only problem with that was I had no other job lined up and rent, bills and food needed to be paid for. I had to decide what was more important, my health and my sanity or my job. There would be no contest so, I handed in my notice and began to look for another job.

Chapter Fifteen

'Street fighting man...'

Much to my relief, I eventually left my position at the Home Office. On paper it was a good job, a career possibly, but due to my issues with the manager, I had to leave. I'm not someone who stays somewhere if I'm not entirely happy. This has been the case throughout every aspect of my life. Sometimes things have worked out well; sometimes they haven't gone to plan. I don't regret things either way because if I didn't try, how would I know if it would work or not. Hindsight is a marvellous thing, it's easy to look back and think 'why did I do that?' but nobody does something under the impression it will fail from the start. Everything you choose is relevant to what's happening in your life at that moment. Would I have left Swansea Rugby Club if I'd known that I would be walking away from the biggest chance I would ever get again? Probably not, but at the time I believed in myself, in my ability that I could still be a success elsewhere. Maybe I could have made it had I stayed or maybe I still would have had the injuries I've had since and it wouldn't have made a blind bit of difference anyway. Would my band have made it big had I carried on with that instead? Possibly, but probably not, the music industry has dramatically changed to when we dreamed of being big. Would I still choose to leave my ex? Of course I would, its making these choices that led me to my best friend, the love of my life and mother to my little boy. Life is fine lines, timing, chances, fate, and luck; call it what you will, but things sometimes happen for a reason.

I decided to apply for my door license badge. I had already completed the course a few years previously. I'd scanned all the job sites, and door work was in abundance. It also paid reasonably well, the only downside appeared to be the late hours. I applied for a job I had seen online, door supervision work, Liverpool city centre, minimum ten hours a week, more for the right applicant and ten pound an hour. I got call back within an hour asking me to come into the office for an interview. I went along and was asked to fill out a few forms. An older gentleman appeared, looked me up and down and said, "Yeah, you fit the criteria. Can you work this weekend?" Knowing what I know now, I'm not exactly sure what 'The criteria' was exactly because they employed some boys who resembled those poor souls you see on a humanitarian famine appeal. I think the only criteria were as long as you're not confined to a wheelchair or registered blind. If you had a valid door badge then you're good to go. All the same, I was delighted to be back in work, if not slightly apprehensive about what I'd actually be doing. Liverpool does have a reputation when it comes to serious incidents. I was told I'd be working in a nightclub named MODO on the notorious Concert Square on the Thursday night. I was unsure where this club was so typed the same into a search engine. I was less than optimistic when I read that a doorman had been stabbed in the neck only three months prior. I think it's common to have a certain degree of apprehension on your first day of work, mine was definitely heightened. I arrived at the venue and was surprised to find it relatively quiet. I was given my radio and ear piece and told to stand outside. In a nutshell, these were the main duties of the position. It was a simple job. Check identification - if they look young, stop them coming in. If they look like shit, stop them coming in and basically keep the peace. Amazingly, certain doormen have trouble adhering to these three simple rules. On my very first night, there was an incident at the bar next door. A young man of about eighteen was being abusive to the door staff and he was chased off the square. He came back a short time later with a knife. Again, he was chased but managed to get away. I didn't relish the realistic danger of potentially being stabbed but I enjoyed my first night. As I was new, I was moved from bar to bar. I was asked to work Christmas Eve at a student bar. I arrived at 8pm and it was already packed. You couldn't move. The floor was covered in little silver metallic objects; legal highs. Out in the beer garden, groups of youths were selling cocaine. There was no control whatsoever and it soon became apparent why. Certain doormen that night were also selling drugs. I was approached and asked if I wanted any 'Lemo' I innocently replied that I was fine with my Red Bull. It turns out that 'Lemo' was a slang name for cocaine. I definitely wasn't down with the kids, thankfully. Into the New Year and I continued to work at various establishments. I even worked security for Liverpool Football Club at Anfield, during the game against eventual champions Leicester City. This might sound reasonably exciting but my duties were to sit near a fire exit and make sure nobody used it before, during or after the match, unless of course it was in the event of an emergency. For twelve hours, I rose to the challenge, put my training to good use and made sure not one person made use of that fire exit. The security manager approached me towards the end of my shift, I was sure I would be commended for my role. Instead, he asked me to escort the manager and players back to their car. This was like a mini promotion and I duly went about my job of escorting Jurgen Klopp and Courthino back to their luxury vehicles, safely protecting them from the dozen or so young children who had been waiting around in the freezing cold to get an autograph or just a glimpse of their idols. One night I was asked to work on the nightclub at the Hilton Hotel. An exclusive club, which basically means it's full of wannabe gangsters and pretentious WAG types. Most of the punters were drinking Grey Goose vodka which costs around £100. I would be content with a bottle of Russian Standard Vodka for £7.99, but each to their own. I was asked by a grey haired man who was trying too hard to keep the remembrance of his youth, to tell the manager he was there. I asked him, "Who should I say it is?" He looked at me before enquiring, "You really don't know who I am?" He seemed a bit perplexed that I genuinely didn't know who he was. It later turned out that this fella is the brother of ex-international footballer, Gary Lineker, so basically, a nobody. To me anyway. He was also joined by the son of George Best, who is also, apparently, famous for being the son of George Best. Later on in the night he approached me to apologise if he came across as rude earlier and gave me £50. I guess he wasn't a bad bloke after all. I've still no idea who he is though.

I'd been working on the doors for a few weeks, things were going well and I hadn't been stabbed at least. I received a call from the boss of the company asking would I be interested in becoming the head doorman at the Walkabout on Concert Square. I think I was offered the position as I had a distinct advantage over most of the men who work on the doors; I could actually communicate with people, not the usual two grunts and a hefty punch. I accepted and started that weekend. The Walkabout had a terrible track record and was almost closed down due to trouble involving the previous security company. I had met with the manager to set out our policies and procedures. We differed from other bars and clubs in the area, in that we allowed large groups of men, stag parties and hen parties and there wasn't a dress code as such. Other bars had a strict no designer labels policy. I found this quite ridiculous really, I mean, I could hardly let someone dressed as a giant chicken in the bar, and then knock the person behind back for wearing a Hugo Boss Polo shirt. It was down to my discretion really. A few weeks in and things were going as well as can be expected. We'd had visits from the licensing authorities and they were happy with the bars performance. The biggest problem faced with most pubs and clubs these days is drugs and our bar was no exception. The use of cocaine is widespread throughout, not just Liverpool, but the UK, and on most nights even on quiet week days, you would be dealing with drug users. It doesn't help that outside the bars are young boys, younger than sixteen, selling anything from legal highs to pills to cocaine. They are obviously working for the main dealer who is never too far away in a flash car; all this is under the nose of the police, who do nothing. It's a ridiculous situation but such is modern society. During the week days, it was a two man door, always a man named Ian with myself. Ian was quite possibly, one of the strangest people I ever met, if not strange then misunderstood and I certainly didn't understand his behaviour. We actually got on quite well; you get to know a lot about someone after standing together for six hours a night. His downfall would be him believing that he was James Bond or some other secret agent. He told me one evening that he was a descendant of the Egyptian god Horace and that he had special blood to prove it. I didn't know whether to bow down to this apparent royalty or stare blankly in confusion. In the end, I did the latter. One time, I watched him walk around the club, talking into, what I assumed was his radio. I walked over and told him that I couldn't hear his messages. His reply dumbfounded me. He said, "Oh, I haven't got a radio; I was talking into my jacket. I just wanted people to think I was talking to back up in case it kicks off.' This wouldn't have been so bad if I hadn't looked around and seen that the bar was completely empty but for seven older women, finishing off their half a lager after the bingo.

I enjoyed the job. It was the closest I had been to a team environment since my rugby days. Plus I enjoyed working in a role where there was a sense of danger. I had to keep on my toes. My first incident of note occurred a few weeks into my new role. It was quite early in the night, one of the boys had gone in to have a word with a stag do that were being too rowdy. Moments later, the doors flew open and my colleague was falling backwards off the steps, grappling with another man. I jumped down to help him and then looked up as six or seven of the stag party piled out of the club. It's hard to describe the moment you are caught up in this situation, you know you are outnumbered and will no doubt get a beating. Time seems to almost turn into slow motion until your natural instinct to protect yourself kicks in. I caught one with a decent punch. As I turned around, I was aware that I myself was being lined up for a smack. What follows next was like something from a Western movie. As I braced for the impending punch, the man who was aiming directly at me was himself, smashed to the floor, as were his remaining friends. There were crumpled bodies in a heap all around. Luckily for us, the door staff from the pub opposite had seen the brawl and got there in the nick of time. For all the faults certain door staffs have, there is definitely a fantastic camaraderie amongst the profession. Most know the importance of backing a colleague up in trouble, and if they don't, they'll soon be hounded out. One night, a group of older women left the bar to go across the road to an outside terrace. All were in good spirits as they left. A few minutes later I noticed a commotion from the same table of women who had just left our bar. Myself, and doormen from a different bar went to see what the problem was. One of the women was now flat on her back, not responding. I can tell you in that situation, panic sets in. An ambulance was called for and her friends were naturally hysterical at the sight of their friend prone on the cold floor. I'm not medically trained so I looked on feeling useless; we all did, we couldn't do anything to help really. A young man, who was on a night out with a stag party came forward and asked did we need help. We asked if he knew first aid and he replied he did. Without hesitation we pushed him towards the casualty. He proceeded to examine her and informed us that she was effectively dead as no pulse could be found. He seemed ridiculously calm, considering what he had just told us. He performed CPR on the unfortunate women for a few moments and was able to get a faint pulse back. He also spoke to the ambulance crew before they arrived informing them of her medical conditions from records he had found on the phone. He even told them what drugs the women would require when they arrived. He was literally a life saver as he took control of the entire situation in a calm manner. The ambulance arrived and I'm told the lady survived. We asked him was he a doctor to which he replied, "No. I'm a medic with the Royal Marines." What are the chances of that? We later learnt that due to the woman's existing medical problems, without that man's intervention at that moment, she would have certainly died before the ambulance arrived. Talk about being in the right place at the right time.

As much as I enjoyed my time on the doors, it was becoming a problem with my home life as for five nights of the week I'd leave Kathryn at home with the baby, not returning until the early hours. It wasn't fair on Kathryn, plus I was missing out on the baby, who, by now, was starting to walk. I'd sleep through most of the days as well, so we were seeing less and less of each other. By chance, I'd got to know one of the door staff opposite my bar. I'd mentioned to him that I'd previously worked for the Home Office and was looking for full time work with normal hours. He told me he worked for the NHS. He was a security manager at a secure mental health unit. He said if any jobs come up, he'd let me know. Luckily for me, I didn't wait too long. I was told about a position in a medium secure psychiatric unit. With a bit of help, I was guided through the application process, into the interview stage and from there I was offered the job. My days of working on the doors, were coming to an end.

Chapter Sixteen

'Looks like we've made it to the end...'

I think it's fitting that at the start of the book, I mentioned a song from a band that would change my teenage years. The song in question was 'Columbia' by Oasis. The opening words to that song are 'There we were; now here we are.' It seems poignant as looking back; things have changed, quite dramatically. My dreams from then have faded but new hopes have been born, quite literally. I can't say I was disappointed to be leaving the door work, I did enjoy certain elements but door work does bring uncertainties. You can't guarantee your own safety as more often than not, it's the actions of others that decide if you have a quiet night, or if there is an incident. Not long after I left, a doorman was stabbed to death in St Helens; it's a realistic danger of the job. You upset people on a daily basis, either by removing them from the premises or not letting them in to start with. Most have a little moan and leave with no issues, however, there is always that one person who takes exception and takes it personally. The actions of that particular person were sadly fatal on this occasion, though after seeing the levels of physical abuse door staff have to put up with, it didn't surprise me. It's a thankless job at times, sometimes dangerous and always eventful. I had Kathryn at home with the baby. They are my priority now. My initial struggles with the baby have most certainly gone. Ethan is coming up to two years of age now and there is nothing better than seeing him develop, learning new things and seeing his own unique personality grow and shine through. As I mentioned, he's now walking extremely well. He loves being outdoors exploring and will literally scream the place down if you threaten to bring him in. He loves the cartoon, Postman Pat and we have the series on a continuous loop from the moment he gets up to the time he goes to sleep. Like most boys, he enjoys playing with mini cars and has a lot of cuddly toys of which he is very particular. Kathryn and I watch and laugh as he examines his toy box and will scrutinise each cuddly before which one makes it back in the box and which one can be left out. He will also be a page boy for Kathryn's sister, Fran's, wedding over in Ireland this summer.

Hopefully, he will be talking by then as he is still trying to form words, though he is a very clever little man and understands questions well. It's easy to get carried away and almost wish his little life away to a more advanced stage but seeing the innocence of children is something amazing and to be treasured. He truly is the greatest thing to ever happen to me. I'm sure I'll look back on this in ten years' time and wonder where the time went because looking back on my own life; I'm not exactly sure where those thirty two years have gone. I still have a lot I want to do, individually, as a couple and of course, as a family. I still have ambitions to get involved in rugby in some capacity, be it coaching or playing socially. I'd be thrilled if I had the opportunity to train my son's future team, if he decides to take up rugby that is, or even better, play alongside Ethan one day, though that may be pushing things. I think becoming a rock star was a more plausible dream. In my working life, I'm fortunate enough to be working for the NHS. I'm restricted in what I can say about the position due to the nature of the secure psychiatric unit. As a couple, obviously getting married is our priority. Neither of us wants a big church wedding, as even though I attended a catholic school and we have both been christened, neither of us believes ourselves to be religious but we will of course let

Ethan make his own choice on what he believes in the future. We want a wedding abroad, the sun, family and friends, good food and plenty to drink. Hopefully soon we will have more children; we have discussed this already, though one Ethan is most definitely enough at the moment. Building a proper family home is another priority. Neither of us thinks that where we are living now is where we see ourselves long term. But as with most things, it takes time. It's fair to say, I'm a different man from the one back in the day. As the saying goes, 'If you view the world at thirty, as you did at twenty, you have wasted ten years of your life.' I find this to be very true. I'm not as wild, almost reckless anymore, though that may have something to with the fact that I very rarely drink. Instead of the wild nights out, it's definitely cosy nights in. I'm not quite a pipe and slippers man just yet though.

Of my family, my parents are now both happily retired and I'm grateful that they frequently make the long journey up to Liverpool to see Me, Kathryn and the baby, though in reality, I'm sure they just want to see the baby and who could blame them? I look forward to seeing them more with every visit. My brother John, still works at the steel works. He is married to Terian and has four children, Cory, Lauren, Joseph and Poppy. My other brother Michael, also works at the steel works. He is in a relationship but as of yet, has no children. Of my friends, Adam is now a fully qualified teacher and has recently entered into a new relationship with Natalie. Adam deserves to find someone he can settle down with and be truly happy. He is a great dad to his young son, Jude and I couldn't think of a better person for a child to look up to. Hopefully one day, Ethan and Jude will have the same friendship as Adam and I had back in the day, maybe without the wayward behaviour and magic mushrooms though. Hibbard currently lives in Gloucester and as mentioned, is married to Louise and they have 3 children together. Two girls and the latest arrival being a little boy named, Jaxson. I know Hibbz was desperate for a son so I was delighted for them when they found out. Jaxson has a lot to live up to. I don't mean in terms of rugby ability, I meant in following in his dads footsteps as a child of running into lampposts at full sprint and bouncing off completely unaffected. Patrick Oliver is still living up in the North East. It was great to catch up with him last summer during the football European Championships in which Wales got to the semi-final. I had not seen Patrick for some 15 years or more. His angelic looks have been replaced by a Viking appearance, with bald head and beard combination. Patrick's partner is also expecting a baby in the next few months. Who knows, maybe our children will pick up where we left off and form their own band and hopefully succeed where we failed. Richie Care is due to be married this summer and is still rocking it on the guitar having had a good experience in the band, Small Tree Down with Adam. Michael Mulhern is currently living in Luxembourg with his girlfriend. He has done fantastically well for himself after promotion through the company, Amazon. I find it equally impressive and terrifying to think that my friends, the very same ones who once caused carnage wherever they went, now hold important roles in various jobs through different sectors. I look back on all these memories and events and smile and as I've said, I regret nothing. I don't look back at these stories and feel it's a life now lost, I look back at it as a life in gained experience, experience that I can pass on to Ethan, experience that will hopefully hold him in good stead for things to come. Ultimately, he will live his own life and make his own mistakes, just as I have. Seeing Ethan so small, so innocent, the gut instinct is to wrap him up in cotton wool and hide him away from the harsh realities of life. Especially with the way the world is at the moment. Deep down I know this is not a realistic possibility. But we as parents can do our best to give him the best start in life, which I know we both will. I feel absolutely privileged to have Kathryn by my side through all this as I couldn't have asked for a better mother for my child, or a better partner to share the rest of my life with. Without the people mentioned throughout the book, my life wouldn't have been what it was and I thank each and every one of you, whatever role you have played.

It's not the days in your life, it's how much life is in your days, and by fuck, we've had some days.

(Below) Kathryn and Me

(Above) No longer looking back, we're only looking forward.

There are places I'll remember
All my life, though some have changed
Some forever, not for better
Some have gone and some remain
All these places have their moments
With lovers and friends I still can recall
Some are dead and some are living
In my life, I've loved them all.